CONTENTS

INTRODUCTION

Pruning is a valuable skill that seems much more complicated than it really is. All pruning affects plant growth, whether you are removing a dead branch, eliminating growth that crowds the center of a plant, or cutting back a shrub. A few basic rules of plant biology govern the effects a pruning session has on growth, and understanding those rules will make you a much more successful, confident, and effective pruner.

Complexity arises because pruning affects both plant species and individual plants differently. Not only does the best time to prune vary from species to species, but some species can tolerate certain types of pruning while others cannot.

Plants also serve various purposes in the landscape, and purpose dictates the need for different pruning approaches. It is no wonder that figuring out where to cut and what to cut is a huge challenge. There are pruning techniques to promote flowering, create a dense plant for screening, cover an arbor, highlight ornamental bark, manage out-of-control growth, and more. Fortunately, all are based on the same aforementioned fundamental rules of plant biology.

The fundamental rules of effective pruning are simple. This book will help you master the essential aspects of pruning and develop a plan for pruning the plants in your landscape. Almost more important, though, are the simple rules that will help you avoid the need to prune at all.

Part 1, Pruning Techniques and Tools, presents information on the basic biology that underlies a plant's reaction to pruning and directions on how to make and use proper pruning cuts. You will also find a guide to pruning tools and suggested pruning goals. The techniques can be applied to every plant you prune. Throughout, you will find suggestions for reducing the amount of pruning your plants need to look their best. Part 2, Pruning Plant by Plant, includes lists that provide details on what a great many trees, shrubs, fruit crops, roses, and vines require to look or yield their best.

PART ONE

PRUNING TECHNIQUES AND TOOLS

Once you understand the basic principles of pruning — why plants react as they do to pruning and how to make proper pruning cuts — you are well on your way to being able to prune any plant, even if you are not sure of its identity. You will also be able to tell when pruning is *not* needed.

The basics of good pruning are the same whether you are attending to a tree, a shrub, or any other woody plant. Although the sizes, angles, and appearance of **stems** and branches vary, proper pruning cuts remain the same. The best first steps are the same as well: Identify and remove dead, diseased, and damaged wood. Next, eliminate rubbing and crossing branches. The key is to learn to effectively use the techniques presented here to foster a healthy plant with sound structure and an attractive shape.

PRUNING AND PLANT GROWTH

PRUNING IS MUCH MORE than cutting off a dead or broken tree limb or chopping back a foundation plant. Every pruning cut affects the future health, growth, and shape of the plant. Do not let this statement scare you away from tackling this essential task altogether. Instead, use it to inspire a sense of serious purpose when you pick up a pair of shears or a saw. Taking the time to prune promptly and properly helps a plant stay healthy and vigorous. Making random cuts at the wrong time of year or in the wrong place can ruin a plant's shape, eliminate this year's flowers or fruit, or cause wayward growth to shoot off in all the wrong directions.

Poor or misguided pruning also can create a plant that requires constant pruning attention. Despite the fact that a great many gardeners prune to make plants smaller, pruning actually promotes growth. In general, **hard pruning** encourages growth; in other words, the more severely you prune a plant, the more vigorously the plant responds with new growth. While intensively managed plants — fruit trees are one example — do end up smaller than their unmanaged relatives, this is the result of repeated pruning sessions. Badly pruned plants generally respond by producing excessive amounts of vegetative growth, making them larger than their unpruned counterparts. Excessive vegetative growth also means fewer or no flowers and often an unattractive and unruly shape.

Understanding the basic biology that underlies plant responses to pruning will help you make good pruning choices.

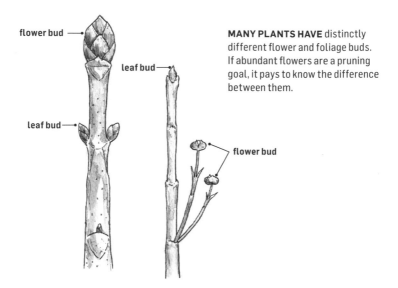

flower bud

leaf bud

leaf bud

leaf bud

flower bud

MANY PLANTS HAVE distinctly different flower and foliage buds. If abundant flowers are a pruning goal, it pays to know the difference between them.

How Wounds "Heal"

"Healing" is not really the correct word to describe the process that helps a tree recover from a pruning wound or damage caused by Mother Nature. Tree wounds never heal. Evidence of every wound, infection, and injury remains written in the wood of a tree throughout its life. Instead, damaged tissue is compartmentalized or sealed off to prevent disease agents from having access to the rest of the plant. As gardeners, it is our job to make the compartmentalization process as easy and as quick as possible. To help trees and shrubs compartmentalize wounds quickly, we need to take the following steps:

Cut off branches at the main trunk or where the branch joins another branch. These are called **thinning cuts**. Always make clean cuts, and do not damage the **branch collar** or leave living or dead **stubs** attached to the plant. (See pages 16 and 19 for directions on making proper thinning cuts.)

To encourage branching, make cuts just above a bud or pair of buds. These are called **heading cuts.** Do not leave a stub above the **bud**, as this will provide access for disease agents. (See page 21 for directions on making proper heading cuts.)

Prune at the proper time of year. See the plant lists in part 2 for timing.

Train trees when they are still young. This establishes good structure and prevents the need to make large pruning wounds later in the tree's life. Small wounds "heal" faster than large wounds, and wounds in young plants and young wood "heal" faster than they do in **old wood.**

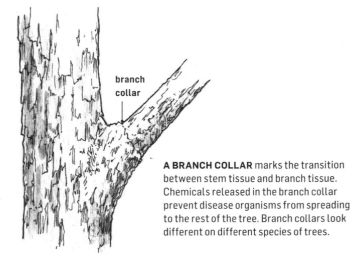

branch
collar

A BRANCH COLLAR marks the transition between stem tissue and branch tissue. Chemicals released in the branch collar prevent disease organisms from spreading to the rest of the tree. Branch collars look different on different species of trees.

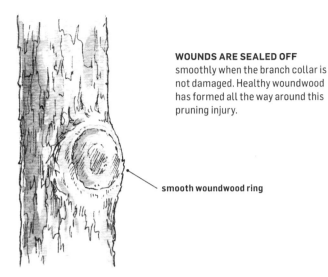

WOUNDS ARE SEALED OFF smoothly when the branch collar is not damaged. Healthy woundwood has formed all the way around this pruning injury.

smooth woundwood ring

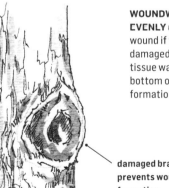

WOUNDWOOD DOES NOT FORM EVENLY all the way around the wound if the branch collar is damaged. Here, vital branch collar tissue was removed at the top and bottom of the cut, preventing the formation of a protective barrier.

damaged branch collar prevents woundwood formation

Do not overprune. On healthy trees, remove 25 percent *or less* of the tree's canopy per year. Prune unhealthy or declining trees even less — pruning is stressful. Topping and other pruning methods that remove more than 25 percent of a tree's canopy damage the tree and cause decline.

Do not use wound dressing on pruning wounds. Although wound dressing was once considered a pruning essential, research has shown that paints and sealers do not prevent decay (some actually foster it) and do not speed recovery from wounds.

Timing

Pruning during the dormant season has a different effect on plant growth than pruning during the growing season. Pruning of any kind causes stress, which is why careful pruning at the right time and for the right reasons is important. Here are some of the factors to keep in mind when timing a pruning project:

Nitrogen/carbohydrate balance. Pruning removes stored carbohydrates, and for evergreens and other plants pruned in summer, it also removes the leaves, which produce carbohydrates. This affects the plant's nitrogen/carbohydrate balance. The changed relationship — less carbohydrate and more nitrogen — encourages vegetative growth (stems and leaves) rather than reproductive growth (flowers and fruit). Root pruning, in contrast, increases the amount of carbohydrates in relation to nitrogen in the plant, thereby increasing flowering or fruiting.

Dormant-season pruning. Trees are especially affected by dormant-season pruning because they store energy (carbohydrates) over the winter in the trunk and roots. Shrubs store energy in their roots, crown, and (to a lesser extent than trees) aboveground stems, so they react somewhat differently than trees do. If a tree's top growth is pruned too heavily, the stored carbohydrates, the amount of which remains relatively unchanged, cause the tree to respond with a growth spurt once the growing season begins. With the same amount of energy, but fewer outlets (branches) to receive that energy, the branches that remain grow more than they would have if the tree were unpruned. This primarily fosters vegetative growth instead of wood that produces flowers and fruit.

Growing season pruning. Pruning during the growing season eliminates leaves, which are an energy source. This tends to slow the growth of the plant. Use thinning cuts in summer to

Prune Hard for Growth

Pruning can be counterintuitive. On a plant with lopsided growth, remember this rule: To encourage weak branches to grow more vigorously, prune them hard; to slow down the growth of already vigorous branches, prune them lightly if at all. Weak, spindly branches will not produce many flowers or fruit and therefore should not be left intact. Rampant growth tends to be primarily vegetative, meaning it produces lots of foliage and branch length, but few flower buds and thus little fruit. Your goal should be to balance growth across the entire plant.

remove **watersprouts** and other excessively vigorous vegetative growth produced during the current season. To minimize winter injury, stop pruning by midsummer to make sure that all new growth has a chance to harden off before the dormant season begins.

Timing rule of thumb. Part 2 of this book contains specific timing recommendations for a wide variety of plants. If you don't know the name of the plant you are pruning, use this simple rule from biologist and plant pathologist Dr. Alex Shigo: "Avoid pruning when leaves are forming or in the fall when they are coloring and dropping." That will not keep you from pruning a plant that **bleeds** at the wrong season, but it will keep you from harming your plants.

Apical Dominance

The bud at the apex, or top, of a young tree or at the tip of any shoot exhibits an effect called **apical dominance** that influences the way the rest of the plant or shoot grows. Called the **apical bud**, it grows more vigorously than other buds farther down the stem, and it also releases plant compounds called auxins that inhibit buds farther down the stem from sprouting. The amount of influence varies: the bud at the tip of a young, unpruned sapling generally exhibits more apical dominance than a bud on the tip of a **side shoot**, for example. Apical dominance also varies among species: it is strong in some and has less influence in others.

Pruning techniques are strongly tied to apical dominance. Cutting off the top of a sapling or the tip of a shoot eliminates

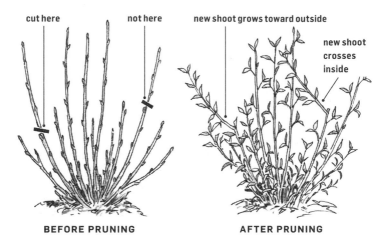

new shoot
crosses
inside

BEFORE PRUNING   **AFTER PRUNING**

ALWAYS CUT JUST ABOVE a bud that is pointing in the direction that you want new shoots to grow.

the auxins that the top bud was releasing. When the topmost bud is removed, the bud that is immediately below the removed tip generally becomes the new dominant bud, although several buds toward the top of the new stem also can begin to grow and compete with one another. The new dominant bud (or several buds competing for dominance) begins to excrete auxins that influence growth farther down the stem.

Apical dominance is the reason it's important to prune above a bud that is *pointing in the direction you want new growth to grow.* If you make pruning cuts above buds that are pointing toward the center of the plant, new growth will result in branches that crowd the center. If you clip above outward-pointing buds, new

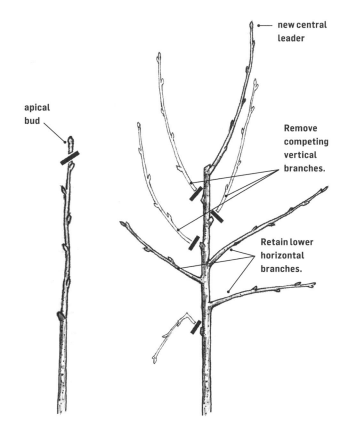

apical
bud

new central
leader

Remove
competing
vertical
branches.

Retain lower
horizontal
branches.

CLIPPING OFF THE BUD at the tip of a shoot causes one or more buds lower on the stem to grow. If a young tree needs a new leader, select the healthiest branch and remove competing vertical branches. Leave branches with a more horizontal orientation, lower on the main stem, to form a framework.

growth will grow outward. Note that in some species, leaf buds can be very small, so look closely.

Keep apical dominance in mind when shaping trees. If the apical bud at the tip of a tree's main stem, or **leader**, is damaged or removed, remaining buds or branches at the top of the tree will begin to compete with one another for dominance, resulting in several vertical branches. If left unpruned, these vertical branches will result in **codominant stems**, often joined to the main leader by weak, narrow **crotches**, or **branch angles**. To reestablish a central leader, select one of the competing branches and use thinning cuts to remove its competitors. Retain branches farther down the stem that have wider, stronger crotch angles to establish a branching framework for the tree. Cut these branches back by one-third to one-half if they are vigorous and might compete with the central leader.

Here are some other effects of apical dominance to keep in mind:

Horizontal branches exhibit less apical dominance than vertical ones. Tying a branch down so that it is at a more horizontal angle lessens the effects of apical dominance. For example, tying vines so that they run horizontally along wires or training the branches of a fruit tree so that they are horizontal, or nearly so, encourages the production of flowers and fruit.

Apical dominance is strongest in young plants and young shoots. As trees near maturity, they tend to branch more as apical dominance lessens. This allows the production of flowers and fruits or seeds.

PRUNING CUTS

THERE ARE TWO TYPES OF PRUNING CUTS: thinning cuts and heading cuts. Both are used whether you are pruning a tree, a shrub, or any other plant. They have different effects on plant growth, and both can be used badly or well. For the best pruning results, think about the proper way each cut is made as you work, and make each cut carefully.

Thinning Cuts

Nearly all of the pruning cuts you will need to make are thinning cuts. These remove a branch or stem by cutting it off at the point where it originated, meaning where it joins to the trunk of a tree or any other branch. By using thinning cuts to remove stems, side branches, or entire branches, you follow a plant's growth pattern and produce plants that look the most natural and require the least amount of pruning maintenance.

Thinning cuts are the appropriate choice for removing dead or diseased branches and for eliminating branches that rub one another or that cross the center of the plant. Thinning cuts are quite useful for opening up the center of a plant so that the plant receives more light and air; they are also useful for eliminating branches that are growing in an awkward direction.

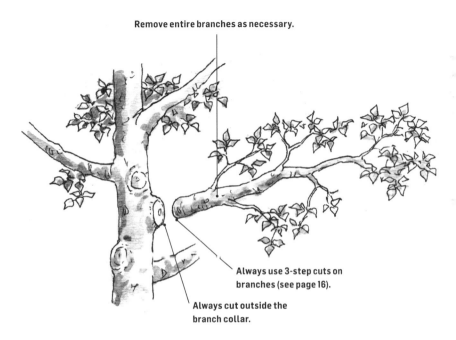

Remove entire branches as necessary.

Always use 3-step cuts on branches (see page 16).

Always cut outside the branch collar.

THINNING CUTS are the best choice In the vast majority of pruning projects.

THINNING CUTS STEP BY STEP

When removing branches from a tree, always use a three-step process to make thinning cuts. Cutting straight through a branch in one go can cause major damage: if the branch falls before the cut is finished, it can tear bark down the trunk. Keep in mind that removing branches when they are still small is best for the tree, as small wounds compartmentalize quicker than large wounds do.

Before you cut, identify the branch collar and the branch bark ridge, which mark the location of the branch core within the tree (see illustration on facing page). Make all cuts outside the branch collar and the branch bark ridge, both of which should be left intact for proper wound compartmentalization.

1. Make a shallow cut on the bottom of the branch, about 12 inches outside the branch collar. This prevents the branch from falling and tearing bark down the trunk while it is being cut.

2. Cut off the branch, this time from the top, about 2 inches outside the first cut.

3. To remove the remaining part of the branch, cut from the top just outside the branch collar.

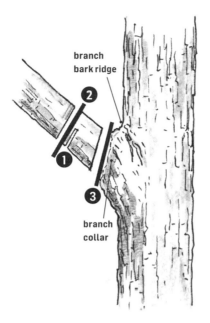

branch
bark ridge

❷

❶

❸

branch
collar

A PROPER THREE-STEP THINNING CUT ensures a clean wound just outside the branch collar and branch bark ridge.

When pruning shrubs or removing small tree branches that arise from other branches, use a small pruning saw, bypass loppers, or bypass hand pruners (depending on the size of the branch being removed) to clip off the branch outside the branch collar. The branch collar is more difficult to see in shrubs and small branches than in large tree branches, but cuts that leave it intact will allow the plant to compartmentalize the wound most effectively.

If you are using bypass loppers or bypass hand pruners (see page 35), position the tool so that the wide, convex cutting blade is next to the main branch. This ensures that your cut is made just outside the branch collar. If the narrow, concave bottom blade is next to the main stem, the cut you are making will be slightly outside where you intend it to be. Either approach the branch from the opposite direction or turn the tool upside down so that the cutting blade is next to the main stem.

Thinning cuts sometimes cause shoots to form near the cut (severely so if you cut into the branch collar). Watch for these and remove them when they are very young, either by rubbing them off or clipping with pruning shears.

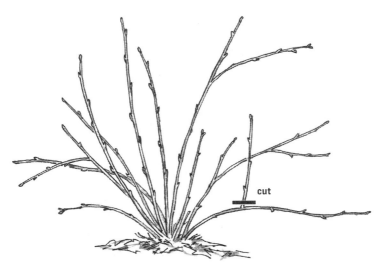

USE THINNING CUTS TO remove branches from shrubs as well. Look closely for the branch collar and cut just outside of it.

Thinning Cut Mistakes

Making flush cuts that damage the branch collar, removing large limbs, and leaving stubs on every cut are all pruning mistakes that make it easy for disease organisms and other problems to invade a tree.

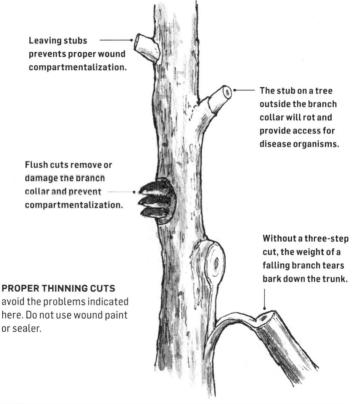

Leaving stubs prevents proper wound compartmentalization.

The stub on a tree outside the branch collar will rot and provide access for disease organisms.

Flush cuts remove or damage the branch collar and prevent compartmentalization.

Without a three-step cut, the weight of a falling branch tears bark down the trunk.

PROPER THINNING CUTS avoid the problems indicated here. Do not use wound paint or sealer.

Plant Choices and Pruning

To reduce the amount of pruning your plants require over their lifetime, consider the following:

- Before you plant, know what size new trees, shrubs, and other plants will reach *at maturity*. To eliminate the need to prune to reduce size, site accordingly. Don't forget to accommodate mature width when planting next to pathways, driveways, other access routes, or other plants. Planting too close to a walkway is a common mistake; plants sited in this manner will need regular pruning to keep them from encroaching on the walkway.

- Do not plant tall trees under power lines. As a general guideline, when planting within 30 feet of a power line, stick to shrubs and trees that are 20 feet or less in height at maturity.

- Train trees and shrubs to foster a shape that is natural for their species. A shrub like forsythia has a natural fountain shape, for example, and it requires far less effort to maintain that shape than it would to maintain a narrow, upright shape or a formal box or rectangle. When selecting a tree for a narrow space, consider one with a fastigiate (with erect branches, nearly parallel to the trunk), columnar, or other upright habit.

- Informal, natural shapes require far less pruning than geometric, formal ones.

- Remove and replace trees and shrubs that require extensive, regular pruning to keep them in bounds.

Heading Cuts

Heading cuts are made across a stem or small branch, above a bud or buds. Heading cuts cause shoots to branch, so they are ideal for encouraging bushy growth to shape a new plant or thicken the density of a hedge. (See Apical Dominance on page 10.) You can also use heading cuts to induce branching to increase the number of stems that might produce flowers, clip off spent flowers, take cuttings for propagation, or shorten overly long stems. Shearing a hedge is a form of making mass heading cuts.

Never use heading cuts to try to reduce the overall size of a plant. Heading cuts induce growth, often vigorous growth, just below the point where the stem tip was removed, quickly replacing lost growth and becoming even larger. This effect is reduced when plants are pruned in the summer, and this is why hedges are often sheared then. Topping a tree is a severe form of using heading cuts that causes excessive growth and an ugly, unsafe framework. In general, use heading cuts only on stems or branches small enough for pruners or loppers. If a saw, or even ratcheting loppers, is required, use thinning cuts instead. Thinning cuts also are the best choice for reducing the size of a plant.

HOW TO MAKE HEADING CUTS

Make heading cuts across a stem about $\frac{1}{4}$ inch above a bud or shoot. Ideally, make each cut so the top of the remaining stem slants away from the bud. The slant directs water away from the cut and reduces incidence of disease. The bottom of the cut should line up with the base of the bud. On plants that bear opposite buds, cut just above a pair of buds or shoots. Make the cut just high enough so that the blade of your pruning tool does not damage the buds.

Always cut just above a bud that is pointing in the direction you want the new growth to go. Generally, this means cutting to a bud that is pointing to the outside of the plant. If you are dealing with pairs of buds, either make sure both buds are pointing in a favorable direction or rub off the bud that is pointing inward.

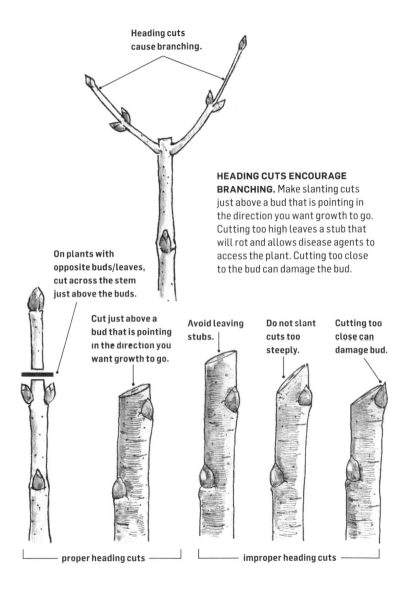

Heading cuts
cause branching.

**HEADING CUTS ENCOURAGE
BRANCHING.** Make slanting cuts
just above a bud that is pointing in
the direction you want growth to go.
Cutting too high leaves a stub that
will rot and allows disease agents to
access the plant. Cutting too close
to the bud can damage the bud.

On plants with
opposite buds/leaves,
cut across the stem
just above the buds.

Cut just above a
bud that is pointing
in the direction you
want growth to go.

Avoid leaving
stubs.

Do not slant
cuts too
steeply.

Cutting too
close can
damage bud.

proper heading cuts

improper heading cuts

PRUNE WITH A PURPOSE

THE BEST FIRST STEP for any pruning session is to make a plan for what you want to accomplish. Pruning without having a particular plan in mind is never a good idea. Start by taking a careful, critical look at the plant you are going to prune. Healthy trees and shrubs that have plenty of room may only need minimal attention, and some may not need any pruning at all.

If the plant that needs to be pruned is near electric lines, or if you need a large tree cut down or large branches cut off, contact a professional arborist to do the job for you. Also contact a professional if you are planning a job that requires climbing a ladder. If you choose to ignore this last piece of advice, at the very least do not climb alone; always work with a partner. (See Jobs for Professionals on page 28 for more pruning jobs that are best left to professionals.)

Mark what you are cutting. Step back and examine the plant from several directions. Then use your observations, together with the objectives listed in the numbered steps that follow, to make a pruning plan for that plant. To keep track of what you need to accomplish, you can mark branches that need to be removed by tying strips of plastic flagging tape on them or spray-painting them.

Jot down a long-term plan. Less is more when it comes to pruning. If a plant needs extensive attention or you are not sure how it will respond, make a pruning plan that extends over several years. Gradual pruning reduces stress on the plant.

Identify which cuts to make this year, which to make next year, and so on. Either make a mental note of your objectives or jot them down in a paper or electronic to-do list.

Go slow. Take your time as you prune. Step back frequently to examine the plant and evaluate your progress. Carefully consider what cuts need to be made next. Don't be afraid either to change your mind about what needs to be removed or to delay some cuts until next season. After all, reattachment is not an option!

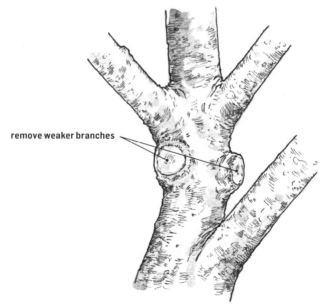

remove weaker branches

LOOK FOR TWO BRANCHES that emerge too close together, and eliminate the weaker of the two.

Step 1: Use Thinning Cuts

Start every pruning operation by using thinning cuts to accomplish these primary objectives:
- Remove dead, dying, diseased, and broken growth.
- Eliminate rubbing and crossing branches by removing the weaker of the two branches.
- Remove branches that cross the center of the plant, especially ones that eventually will rub or will produce side branches that rub. This opens up the center of the plant to light, improves air circulation, and prevents problems later on.
- Prune out other unwanted growth such as **watersprouts** and **suckers**.

Step 2: Continue with Thinning Cuts If Necessary

Depending on the plant, you may need to continue using thinning cuts to achieve the following:
- Reduce the overall size of a shrub, at least temporarily. Use thinning cuts to remove the longest or tallest branch or branches, always cutting back to the branch from which it originated or all the way to the ground.
- Eliminate competing leaders on a young tree. (See the box Competing Leaders on page 54 for more on training young trees.)
- Limb up (remove the lower branches of) a tree if necessary to make room underneath it for plants or people. (On older trees, have this done by a professional.) Do this gradually by removing one or two branches per year. Branches do not

move up a tree as it grows, so remove any that are too close to the ground while they are still small.

- Remove branches to reveal handsome bark or branching habit. Again, remove branches gradually to minimize stress on the plant.
- Cut out growth that has reverted. This means cutting out green-leaved sections that have developed on a plant that otherwise has green leaves variegated with yellow or white. Also remove upright growth on grafted weeping trees. Cut reverted growth back to the point where it originated.
- Renewal-prune by cutting off some of the older stems at the base of the plant or at the point of origin on another branch. (See Regular Renewal Pruning on page 79.)

Step 3: Use Heading Cuts as Needed

Use heading cuts to:

- Cut back branches or branch tips to encourage branching and dense, bushy growth. Remember to cut above a bud that is pointing in the direction you want new growth to go.
- Cut a shrub back to a framework. (See Framework Pruning on page 80.)
- Balance growth by cutting back weak branches hard and vigorous branches lightly or not at all.
- Shear a hedge. (Do not, however, use heading cuts to shear a shrub in an attempt to reduce the overall size.)
- Cut back vines to control the production of flowers or fruit.
- Clip off spent flowers.

Step 4: Use a Combination of Thinning and Heading Cuts as Needed

Use a combination of cuts to achieve the following:

- Reshape or maintain the overall shape of a plant. For example, use both types of cuts to correct the shape of a shrub so that it is wider at the bottom than at the top. This ensures that light reaches the bottom leaves and prevents them from dropping off the plant.
- Remove spent wood, meaning growth that has flowered but will not flower again, or encourage the production of new, more vigorous growth that will produce more abundant flowers or fruit.

JOBS FOR PROFESSIONALS

TREES ARE VALUABLE landscape assets, and it is in your best interest to hire highly qualified professionals to care for them. Top-quality arborists can perform many pruning tasks that homeowners should not attempt, including climbing trees and removing larger branches.

Make the effort to find a highly qualified professional arborist; your trees will thank you. Never hire a self-described "tree trimmer" or a company that happened to cut down trees in a neighbor's yard. Look for established companies that advertise experts certified by the International Society of Arboriculture (ISA), the Tree Care Industry Association (TCIA), or the American Society of Consulting Arborists (ASCA). Membership in an arboricultural association does not guarantee good workmanship, however, so ask for references from customers for whom the arborist has done similar work. Top-of-the line professionals will be happy to put you in touch with their customers. Also confirm that any company you hire has insurance to cover personal and property damage as well as workers' compensation.

Certified arborists can perform any of the tasks listed under Prune with a Purpose on page 24, train young trees, and much more. Here are some additional pruning jobs best left to professionals:

Crown reduction and thinning. Crown reduction is most often used to deal with a tree that has outgrown its allotted space. To reduce the overall size of the crown, the arborist will remove large branches down to the branches they arose from. Also called drop-crotch pruning, this leads to a fairly natural looking crown, although it leaves large wounds that can develop rot. Crown thinning involves removing branches inside the crown to increase air circulation and allow more light to reach the ground. Thinning can also reduce wind resistance. A combination of crown reduction and thinning is much better for a tree than topping, which involves chopping off branches anywhere along their length. Topping leaves a mutilated tree and generally leads to a multitude of suckers at the end of each cut.

Crown lifting. Also called limbing up, **crown lifting** involves removing the lower branches on a tree to provide room for pedestrians or other access.

BEFORE

AFTER

CROWN REDUCTION uses thinning cuts to reduce the overall size of a tree while maintaining a natural-looking shape. It also opens up the interior of the crown to allow more light to reach interior leaves and branches and provide better air circulation.

Tree safety and renovation. Expert arborists can evaluate whether a tree is safe; they can also determine whether an unsafe tree can be repaired or should be removed. To do this, they look for signs of damage, weak branch crotches, **included bark** (bark that has become incorporated into the joint between a branch and the trunk), signs of rot, cracks in the trunk, damaged roots, and other factors that can turn a tree into a hazard. They will know whether lopsided growth can be corrected and, if so, how to do it. They will also know how to spread pruning out over several years to save a tree that has been neglected.

Large branch removal. Professionals have the skills and tools needed to make clean cuts on large branches. They are also able to climb trees safely, so hire them to do any pruning that involves removing branches greater than about 2 or 3 inches in diameter, or anytime using a ladder or climbing a tree is required.

Arborists can also consult and make recommendations on the best pruning options for trees, including removing them; deal with storm damage; and work around buildings, electric wires, and other obstacles.

PRUNING AND SIZE CONTROL

PRUNING CAN BE USED TO REDUCE the size of a plant, but it does so at the expense of maintenance. Properly pruned fruit trees and rosebushes are smaller than their unpruned counterparts, but the plant remains smaller only if it is pruned regularly. Proper pruning also yields thicker, denser growth, because it encourages branching. Still, the fact remains that pruning stimulates growth.

The question to ask yourself is whether the benefits are worth the effort. While some plants need annual pruning to flower or bear well, repeatedly pruning a shrub to keep it from swamping neighboring shrubs or overgrowing a walkway only prevents a problem; it does not really yield benefits. The same is true of trees that have been repeatedly topped in a fruitless attempt to make them into smaller trees. Usually, one resorts to this type of pruning when a plant was badly chosen or not sited properly. Plants pruned only for size control rarely look attractive or are very healthy. The best approach is to replace the plant with a selection that will attain a suitable size at maturity.

When purchasing a plant and deciding where to site it, pay attention to height and width of the plant *at maturity*. Site plants so that they will have adequate space for their entire lives. Also select appropriately sized plants that will fit the size of your landscape. Plants selected and sited in this way, and given good initial training, rarely need more than occasional pruning attention.

TOOLS OF THE TRADE

SHARP TOOLS THAT MAKE CLEAN CUTS are essential for effective pruning. Smooth, clean cuts seal fastest and are least likely to allow disease organisms to enter the plant. It is equally important not to exceed the cutting ability of your equipment. Trying to force a pair of pruning shears to cut a stem that is too thick results in crushed tissue and a ragged cut. Instead, step up to equipment that can easily handle the stem; be ready to switch from hand pruners to loppers, and from loppers to a pruning saw.

Tool Care

Pruning tools appreciate being wiped off after each use with a clean, dry cloth, but most gardeners do this only at the end of the season. Check blades to see if they need sharpening, and send saws out for professional sharpening, if needed.

Pruners, loppers, and other implements can be sent out for sharpening, too, but you can also learn to do this yourself. Alternatively, you can buy replacement blades and other parts so that your tools are ready for action when pruning season comes around again.

Finally, oil tools with a product designed for tool care (WD-40 is fine) and wipe them with a clean, dry cloth. Rub wooden handles with boiled linseed oil. The wooden handles of new tools are typically coated with varnish. Lightly sand them to remove the varnish before applying boiled linseed oil.

Buy the highest-quality tools you can afford. A properly sized tool makes the work easier and less tiring, so handle as many different models as you can to determine which feels comfortable in your hand before you buy. FELCO, the premier brand for hand pruners, offers various models suited to different sizes of hands, plus models for right- and left-handed gardeners.

A number of manufacturers (including FELCO) offer replaceable parts, like blades, which extend the life of the tool. Well-made tools not only make gardening easier; they also are a greener option when compared to equipment that is designed to be tossed out as soon as the blades become dull or parts wear out.

Protect Yourself!

In addition to a good saw and a good pair of hand pruners, be sure to add basic safety gear to your pruning arsenal. Wear gloves and long sleeves for any operation that involves crawling on the ground or dealing with thorny stems. Every gardener should wear eye protection when pruning. Safety glasses will protect you from twigs and branches whipping into your eyes, not to mention sawdust. If you are using a pole saw or pruner, wear protective headgear to guard against falling branches.

Hand Pruners

A pair of top-quality hand pruners is essential equipment for any gardener. In addition to at least one standard pair of hand pruners, most gardeners also acquire a variety of smaller nips or flower shears to use for cutting flowers or trimming off small stems. If you can't afford a top-of-the-line pair of pruners, start saving now or add this item to your wish list.

If properly cared for, a pair of professional-quality pruners, like those offered by FELCO, will last a lifetime. Whatever brand or model you buy, look for models with high-carbon steel blades, replaceable blades and other replaceable parts, and a comfortable grip. Pruners should open and close smoothly, and the latch that keeps them closed for storage should be easy to snap on and off.

Bypass pruners. These work like scissors and have two curved blades. The wide, convex blade is beveled and sharp, and the tool cuts as this blade passes by the narrow, concave

TOP-QUALITY BYPASS HAND PRUNERS are essential equipment that will last a lifetime. Buy a brand that offers replacement parts. The sharp wide cutting blade passes the narrow bill to make a clean, scissorlike cut.

anvil blade. You would normally hold bypass pruners with the convex cutting blade on top. However, depending on where you are standing and the direction of the stem you are cutting, you may need to turn them upside down so that the convex blade remains next to the stem. That way you can make the cut properly without leaving a stub. These are the go-to tools for nipping off branches or stems up to about ½ inch in diameter, depending on how strong your hands are. If you have to struggle at all, step up to ratchet pruners, loppers, or a pruning saw.

Anvil pruners. These cut when the sharp blade is pressed down onto the flattened anvil. Anvil pruners crush tissue when they cut, but they are useful for removing deadwood such as small stems. Bypass pruners are better for live wood because they cut with a slicing, rather than crushing, motion.

Ratchet pruners. These have an internal mechanism that holds the stem, and they cut as the gardener repeatedly squeezes the handle. Available in both bypass and anvil

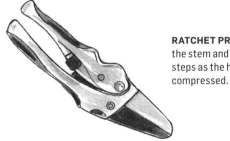

RATCHET PRUNERS grip the stem and tighten in steps as the handle is compressed.

designs, ratchet pruners are useful for gardeners who lack the hand strength to use conventional pruners. Ergonomic pruners also are available, and experimenting with them is worthwhile if hand strength is an issue.

Long-reach pruners. These are pruners with a long handle. Models with 2-foot-long handles make it easy to reach small branches at a distance. Models with 5-foot-long handles are effective pole pruners.

Loppers

Loppers are designed for cutting branches that are too large for hand pruners but too small for a pruning saw. Essentially, they function exactly like hand pruners (both bypass and anvil designs are available), but they have longer handles designed to give the gardener a longer reach as well as greater leverage.

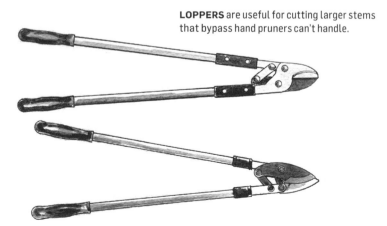

LOPPERS are useful for cutting larger stems that bypass hand pruners can't handle.

Handle length varies from about 14 to 36 inches, and handles are made of hardwood, steel, or aluminum. Blades should be made of steel.

Loppers cut branches up to about 2 inches thick, depending on the model you use and your arm strength. Bypass loppers scissor through stems; anvil types, best for cutting out deadwood, press a sharp blade onto an anvil to cut. If you have to strain at all, switch to a pruning saw or try one of the newer lopper designs with ratchet action or gears that increase power and leverage and thereby allow you to cut wider stems than you can with standard loppers.

Hedge Shears

While electric hedge trimmers are common these days, old-style hedge shears are still valuable for maintaining sheared hedges. They are useful only for maintaining formal hedges; look to other tools for any other pruning jobs. Hedge shears create flat surfaces and straight lines, neither of which are appropriate for most shrubs, where natural shapes and lines are better looking and far less work to maintain.

Hedge shears are designed to cut only young, green stems. Do not use them to cut back into old wood, because they will not cut cleanly and the plant will be very slow to recover from the wounds they inflict. If you do need a pair, look for forged carbon steel blades and hardwood or metal handles that are cushioned for comfortable use. Some models have a wavy-edged blade designed to trap errant stems, while others have a section with a serrated edge for the same purpose. It takes time to learn to use hedge shears correctly, but newer models are easier to use than older shears were.

Pruning Saws

For removing branches, especially in close quarters, a good pruning saw is a must. A great many models are available, and the largest saw is not necessarily the most effective. A good-quality curved-bladed pruning saw can easily fit into tight spaces. A good pruning saw has the following features:

- **Tri-edge teeth**, which have three bevels per tooth. Saws with these cut faster than saws with other tooth patterns.

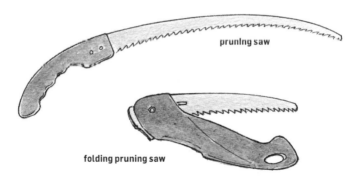

PRUNING SAWS are designed to make clean cuts and work effectively in tight spaces.

- **A curved blade,** which is easiest to use and most efficient.
- **A 12- to 13-inch-long blade** to cut branches up to about 2 inches in diameter. Longer blades, to 20 inches or so, are better for larger branches. You may want one of each.
- **A high-carbon steel blade** that has been hardened and tempered. Many models also feature plated blades that resist rust.
- **A strong, secure blade-to-handle connection.** Wood handles are traditional, but high-impact plastic, often cushioned with rubber to make the grip comfortable and secure, is effective as well.
- **A scabbard** designed to hold your regular pruning saw. (Folding ones don't need a scabbard.) This makes the saw easier to carry and prevents injuries to you and damage to the saw.

You may also want to keep a folding saw in your tool bucket so that it is always handy. Make sure it locks into position, whether closed or open, for safety. Models with 7- to 10-inch blades are common, although longer blades are available.

Pole Saws and Pruners

A variety of cutting tools is available to make it possible to reach tall branches while keeping your feet firmly and safely on the ground. Some have set-length handles, others telescoping ones. There are models with a saw only or a pruner only, as well as ones with both saw and pruner.

While these tools can be useful, try out a model before you buy it. They may be heavier than you think, and controlling them enough to make a clean cut can be a challenge. It is very difficult to make proper three-step cuts while holding a pole saw in the air, so it is easy to do considerable damage to the branch.

Chain Saws

While useful for cutting up limbs that have already fallen off a tree, or cutting up entire fallen trees already on the ground, chain saws are not pruning tools, especially in the hands of amateur gardeners. They are hard to control, making it difficult or impossible to accomplish proper three-step pruning cuts (see page 16). A fine-quality handsaw makes cleaner, more accurate cuts. It is also far less likely to damage nearby limbs or other plant parts. Chain saws are inherently dangerous, even if you have both feet on the ground. Holding one up high in the air to reach a low tree limb, not to mention climbing a ladder with one in hand, is asking for an accident to happen.

To use a pole pruner effectively, you simply have to pull a rope or other mechanism to make the required cuts. Look for a model with a bypass pruner. As with conventional hand pruners, do not try to exceed the cutting power of the tool, or you will leave rough cuts that do not recover quickly. Position the cutting edge carefully, as you would a pair of hand pruners, before making each cut. Pole saws and pruners also can be held horizontally; for example, you can use them to reach into a shrub rose to remove older stems while avoiding thorns.

With either a pole saw or a pole pruner, wear head and eye protection when pruning, because you will be in danger of having sawdust as well as entire limbs fall down on you.

PART TWO

PRUNING PLANT BY PLANT

Proper heading and thinning cuts are universal to any effective pruning operation, and once you understand how and why to use them, you are on your way to becoming an expert pruner. Timing is another variable, since the ideal time to prune a plant varies from species to species. In this part, I provide plant lists with specific information on the best ways to prune a wide variety of popular trees, shrubs, roses, and vines. In addition to information on the best time to prune each of these species, you will also find recommended pruning styles that work for each plant.

PRUNING TREES

MOST ESTABLISHED TREES REQUIRE minimal pruning, but regular attention is important for keeping them healthy and safe. (Apples, peaches, and other crop-bearing fruit trees require careful training and regular annual care. See Pruning Fruit Trees on page 64 for more information on pruning requirements.) Training a young sapling to develop a sound, pleasing structure is the best way to foster a tree that remains attractive, as well as sound and safe, for the rest of its life. Early training also greatly reduces the need to prune when the tree is older. In a young tree, wounds heal quickly and the necessary pruning cuts are smaller, so they also heal faster.

Once trees are mature, pruning is more stressful (since wounds are larger) and also more expensive. Hiring a certified arborist is the best course of action. (See Jobs for Professionals on page 28 for tips on hiring professionals and what work they can do for you.)

Tree Shapes

Choose a pruning style that echoes the natural shape of the tree. Otherwise, you will be fighting the tree's natural shape for its lifetime. If you are purchasing a new tree, buy one that has received initial training. Most young trees will have a clear central leader, or, if multi-stemmed, a leader for each trunk. Make sure branches point out from all directions around the trunk. Also look for wayward branches, forked stems, or overall lopsided growth, all of which indicate poor or no initial training. While these faults can be corrected, you will have fewer problems if you start with a tree that has received proper early pruning.

Before you buy, find out how large a tree will grow — both its height and its spread — and select a spot where its mature size can be accommodated. If you do not have room for the mature tree, look for another species or a compact cultivar that fits your site. While large trees can be contained with severe pruning, and wide-spreading ones can be cut back to accommodate a narrow site, trying to restrain a tree's growth by pruning requires major work and annual attention. Proper selection with siting in mind is not only sensible with regard to maintenance; it also yields healthier, better-looking trees.

....

Be Aware of Invasives

The plant lists in Part 2 include some popular species designated "invasive" in some parts of the country. This means they are non-native plants that reproduce rapidly, escape cultivation, and crowd out native plants. Invasive plants are found in a great many gardens and are included here because they also require pruning. If at all possible, try to replace invasive plants with other species, preferably native ones. Consult your local Cooperative Extension Service or a high-quality local nursery or garden center for lists of invasives that are causing problems in your area. Also ask for replacement suggestions.

....

Staking

Firmly staking newly planted trees was once considered essential. Researchers have since determined that allowing a tree's trunk to flex helps it grow stronger, and many trees do not require staking. Consult your local Cooperative Extension Service, an arborist, or the expert at your local garden center to determine whether the tree you are buying, due to its nature or the conditions of the site you are planning for it, should be staked. Also ask for advice on materials to use and information on how long any stakes should remain in place.

In general, trees should be staked if one or more of the following conditions exist:

- The top growth is large when compared to the size of the root-ball. Wind can blow a top-heavy plant to the extent that roots are prevented from growing out into the surrounding soil.

- The tree will be located on a windy site or one with high traffic. Winds may uproot the tree or cause it to move so much that roots fail to grow into the surrounding soil. High-traffic sites, where the tree may be routinely bumped by passersby, pose similar problems.

- The tree may be uprooted or stolen by vandals.

The following basic tree forms fit a wide variety of species. Prune most trees from winter to early spring, but check the Tree-by-Tree Guide on page 56 for specific recommendations.

SINGLE-LEADER AND FEATHERED TREES

Single-leader trees have a clear trunk that lacks lateral branches, while feathered trees have lateral branches that radiate all the way around the trunk to the ground. Both of these forms have a tall, straight trunk that ends in a main terminal shoot, although once trees age, the crown tends to broaden and the main central leader disappears altogether or is less evident.

The natural shape of many deciduous trees is feathered, and this is also the recommended shape for most broad-leaved evergreen trees, such as American holly (*Ilex opaca*) and Southern magnolia (*Magnolia grandiflora*). Deciduous trees that are used as shade trees in sites where pedestrians or other traffic can fit underneath their branches, such as oaks (*Quercus* spp.) and many maples (*Acer* spp.), are trained as single-leader specimens. Deciduous species trained as feathered trees typically lose their lower branches as they age and their crown broadens.

Pruning year 1: During the first year of training, select a single central leader. Use thinning cuts to remove vertical branches near the top of the tree that have narrow crotch angles and may compete with the central leader. Farther down the stem, select lateral branches that have wide angles to create the main framework of the tree. Use thinning cuts to remove branches that cross other branches or point in awkward directions. If

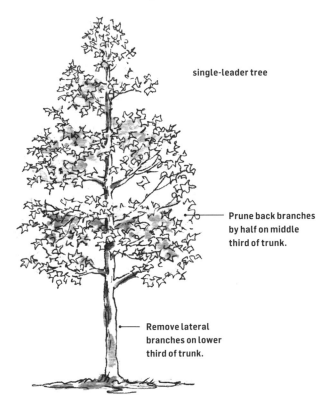

single-leader tree

Prune back branches by half on middle third of trunk.

Remove lateral branches on lower third of trunk.

two or more branches arise too close together, remove the weaker branch or branches.

On feathered trees, remove any lateral growth that arises low enough on the trunk that a branch touches the ground. On single-leader trees, also remove lateral branches on the lower third of the trunk and cut back branches on the middle third of the trunk by about half.

feathered tree

Remove any lateral branches that touch the ground.

Pruning years 2 and 3: On both forms, continue removing rubbing and crossing branches and vigorous vertical branches that threaten to compete with the central leader. On feathered trees, remove any branches that reemerge close to the ground.

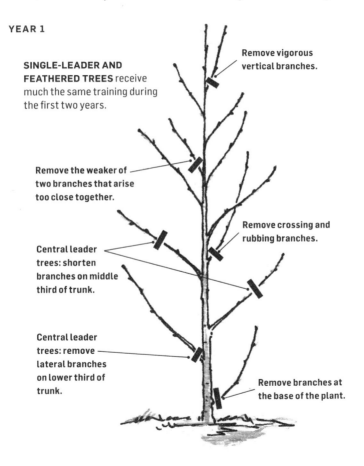

YEAR 1

SINGLE-LEADER AND FEATHERED TREES receive much the same training during the first two years.

Remove vigorous vertical branches.

Remove the weaker of two branches that arise too close together.

Remove crossing and rubbing branches.

Central leader trees: shorten branches on middle third of trunk.

Central leader trees: remove lateral branches on lower third of trunk.

Remove branches at the base of the plant.

On central-leader trees, in year three continue removing lateral branches on the lower third of the trunk and shortening laterals on the middle third.

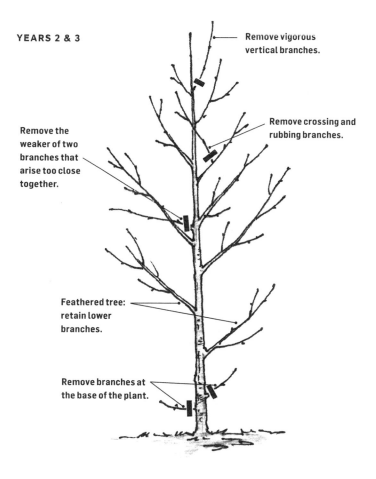

YEARS 2 & 3

Remove vigorous vertical branches.

Remove crossing and rubbing branches.

Remove the weaker of two branches that arise too close together.

Feathered tree: retain lower branches.

Remove branches at the base of the plant.

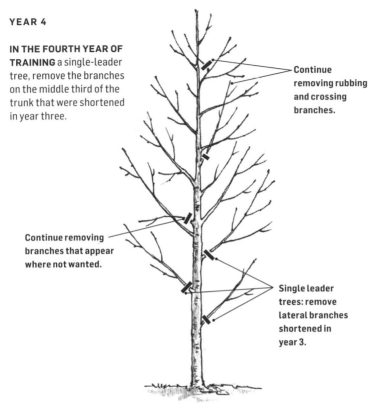

IN THE FOURTH YEAR OF TRAINING a single-leader tree, remove the branches on the middle third of the trunk that were shortened in year three.

Continue removing rubbing and crossing branches.

Continue removing branches that appear where not wanted.

Single leader trees: remove lateral branches shortened in year 3.

Pruning year 4: On single-leader trees, remove branches on the middle third of the trunk.

BRANCHED STANDARD TREES

Branched standard trees have a straight, single trunk topped by a crown of branches. For the first two years, train branched standard trees as you would a single-leader tree. Depending on the ultimate size of the tree, you will want three or four strong lateral branches. The third year, use a thinning cut to remove the central leader. In subsequent years, remove any rubbing and crossing branches, along with any vertical branches that begin to dominate the crown of the tree. Also watch for and eliminate branches that have narrow crotch angles.

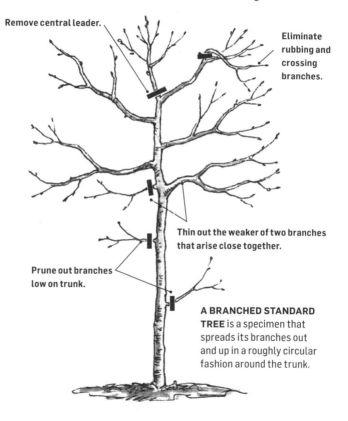

Remove central leader.

Eliminate rubbing and crossing branches.

Thin out the weaker of two branches that arise close together.

Prune out branches low on trunk.

A BRANCHED STANDARD TREE is a specimen that spreads its branches out and up in a roughly circular fashion around the trunk.

Competing Leaders

To create a sound, safe framework for a tree, eliminate leaders that will compete with one another. The sooner you select a main leader and eliminate its competitors, the better, because pruning wounds will be smaller and will compartmentalize more quickly.

ALSO CALLED DUAL LEADERS, codominant leaders compete with one another. They are far easier to fix when a tree is young than when the tree is mature.

Cut outside branch bark ridge.

It is equally important to replace a leader if the main stem of a tree is damaged. If this happens, cut back to a vigorous, upright branch, and tie it firmly but not too tightly to a stake to ensure that it grows in the right direction.

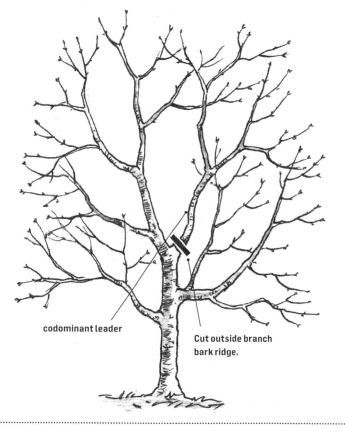

codominant leader

Cut outside branch bark ridge.

Tree-by-Tree Guide

Unless otherwise noted below, most trees are initially trained to a feathered tree or a central leader for the first few years. Good early training is the best way to nurture trees that have minimal pruning requirements at maturity. Also, unless otherwise specified, prune trees from late fall to midwinter, when they are dormant. Dead and diseased wood can be removed in summer. Inspect mature trees at least annually to look for broken, dead, or diseased branches, along with crossing and rubbing growth.

***Acer* spp. (maples).** Prune from late fall to midwinter, when completely dormant. Some species bleed at other seasons. Remove reverted or wayward shoots in late summer or early fall. Several species, including Norway maple (*A. platanoides*), are invasive.

***Aesculus* spp. (buckeyes).** Prune from late fall to late winter.

***Betula* spp. (birches).** Prune only if necessary, and then only from late fall to early winter when plants are completely dormant. Wounds made in other seasons bleed profusely. Birches resent being cut back hard.

***Carpinus* spp. (hornbeams).** Prune from late fall to midwinter when plants are dormant. Wounds made in other seasons will bleed. Plants grown as trees require minimal pruning, but hornbeams can withstand hard pruning and can be grown as hedges. Prune hedges in late summer.

***Carya* spp. (hickories).** Prune from late fall to midwinter when plants are completely dormant. Wounds made in spring bleed profusely. Prune only if necessary.

***Catalpa* spp. (catalpas).** Prune from late fall to early spring.

Celtis spp. (hackberries). Prune from late winter to early spring.

Cercidiphyllum japonicum (katsura tree). Prune from late fall to very early spring. Avoid hard pruning.

Cercis spp. (redbuds). Prune after flowering, if necessary, in early summer. Minimal pruning is best.

Cladrastis lutea (yellowwood). Prune in mid- to late summer to prevent bleeding. Watch for, and eliminate, branches with narrow, weak crotch angles.

Cornus spp. (dogwoods). Prune from fall to early spring. Remove dead branches any time. Minimal pruning is best.

Crataegus spp. (hawthorns). Prune between fall and early spring.

Diospyros spp. (persimmons). Minimal pruning required. A strong framework with broad, strong crotch angles is important to carry fruit crops. Fruit is borne on new wood (growth produced the current season), so prune from late winter to early spring.

Eucalyptus spp. (eucalyptus, gum trees). Prune from fall to early spring, just as new growth begins after danger of hard frost.

Fagus spp. (beeches). Prune from fall to early spring. Minimal pruning is best.

Ficus spp. (figs). Prune any time in frost-free regions.

Fraxinus spp. (ashes). Prune from late fall to early spring.

Ginkgo biloba (ginkgo). Prune from late fall to early spring. Minimal pruning is best.

Gleditsia spp. (honey locusts). Prune from fall to midwinter.

Halesia spp. (silverbells). Prune from late fall to early spring.

Ilex opaca (**American holly**). Prune in mid-spring or trim and shape in mid- to late summer. Aim for a pyramid shape to allow light to reach the lower leaves and prevent them from dropping. Plants tolerate hard pruning, which can be used to encourage dense growth or reduce the overall width of a plant. It is best to spread out hard pruning over several years. Prune to collect branches for holiday decorations in early winter.

Juglans **spp. (walnuts).** Prune from late fall to midwinter. Wounds made later in the season will bleed.

Lagerstroemia **spp. (crape myrtles).** Prune from late fall to early spring. Plants withstand hard pruning, but it's unnecessary to top trees annually for good bloom, and it creates an ugly winter silhouette. Keeping pruning to a minimum creates a more attractive silhouette and reduces maintenance.

Liquidambar styraciflua (**American sweetgum**). Prune from midwinter to early spring.

Liriodendron tulipifera (**tulip tree**). Prune from winter to early spring. Minimal pruning is best.

Magnolias **spp. (magnolias).** Prune only if necessary, as many species bleed. If light pruning or shaping is necessary, proper pruning time depends on when plants flower. For deciduous species that bloom before or with new leaves in spring, remove small branches (½ inch diameter or less) in midsummer after the leaves have fully expanded. Prune summer-blooming magnolias when new growth begins in spring.

Malus **spp. (crab apples).** Prune from fall to early spring. Remove watersprouts in midsummer.

Morus spp. (mulberries). Prune from fall to early winter when fully dormant. Wounds bleed, so avoid pruning after midwinter. White mulberry (*M. alba*) is invasive.

Nyssa sylvatica (tupelo, black gum). Prune from fall to early spring when fully dormant.

Oxydendrum arboreum (sourwood). Prune from fall to early spring when fully dormant. Minimal pruning is best.

Palms. These trees require minimal pruning. Avoid damaging the growth point at the top of the main stem. For clumping species, remove suckers, if necessary, to reduce the size of the clump. Remove dead leaves any time of year by cutting near the base of the leafstalk.

Platanus spp. (sycamores). Prune from fall to early spring.

Populus spp. (aspens, cottonwoods). Prune in late summer to early fall. Many species bleed if pruned in late winter or in spring. Summer pruning helps prevent disease that enters through pruning wounds. White poplar (*P. alba*) is invasive.

Prunus spp. (cherries, plums). Prune only if necessary, and train trees when very young. Prune in midsummer and keep pruning wounds as small as possible to prevent disease transmission.

Pyrus spp. (pears). Prune from fall to early spring. Callery pears (*P. calleryana*, including 'Bradford') typically develop congested branches and weak, narrow crotch angles that break. Select plants and train them to develop well-spaced branches and strong, broad crotch angles. Callery pears (*Prunus calleryana*, including 'Bradford') are invasive.

Quercus spp. (oaks). Prune from winter to early spring when dormant. Prune evergreen oaks in mid- to late summer. Sawtooth oak (*Q. acutissima*) is invasive.

Robinia **spp. (locusts).** Prune in mid- to late summer. Black locust (*R. pseudoacacia*) is invasive.

Salix **spp. (willows).** Prune from fall to early spring when dormant.

Sorbus **spp. (mountain ashes).** Prune in mid- to late summer.

Stewartia **spp. (Stewartias).** Prune in late winter to early spring.

Styrax **spp. (snowbells).** Prune from fall to early spring when dormant.

Syringa **spp. (lilacs).** *See* Pruning Shrubs, page 74.

Tilia **spp. (lindens).** Prune either in midwinter or midsummer. Wounds bleed when plants are pruned at other times of year.

Ulmus **spp. (elms).** Prune from fall to early spring when dormant. Chinese and Siberian elms (*U. parvifolia, U. pumila*) are invasive.

Zelkova **spp. (zelkovas).** Prune in late winter.

....

Multi-Trunked Trees

Also called multi-stemmed or clumping trees, multi-trunked trees have two or more main trunks and range in size from large shrubs to full-size trees. Birches (*Betula* spp.), redbuds (*Cercis* spp.), and some crab apples (*Malus* spp.) are offered as both multi-trunked and single-stemmed specimens. Suckering trees such as sassafras (*Sassafras albidum*) and tupelos (*Nyssa sylvatica*) can be allowed to form clumps.

....

Large shrubs such as blackhaw viburnum (*Viburnum prunifolium*) can be pruned to create small multi-trunked trees: Select the main stems that form the trunk and remove lower lateral branches over the course of two or more seasons.

When pruning multi-trunked trees, remove lateral branches that are close to the ground, along with unwanted suckers. Also use thinning cuts to remove rubbing and crossing branches, to eliminate congestion in the center of the clump, and to open up the plant so that the framework of the tree is visible.

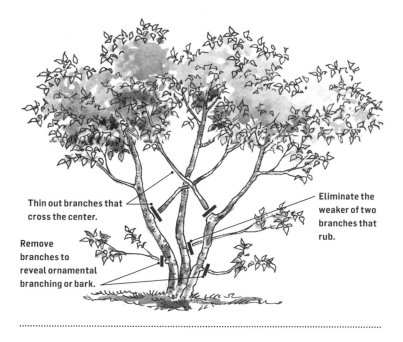

Thin out branches that cross the center.

Remove branches to reveal ornamental branching or bark.

Eliminate the weaker of two branches that rub.

Pruning Conifers

Plants such as firs (*Abies* spp.), pines (*Pinus* spp.), spruces (*Picea* spp.), arborvitaes (*Thuja* spp.), junipers (*Juniperus* spp.), leyland cypress (*Cupressus* x *leylandii*), and hemlocks (*Tsuga* spp.) are collectively called conifers because they bear their seeds in cones. Most are evergreens with needlelike leaves, although some conifers are deciduous, meaning they drop their leaves over winter. Larches (*Larix* spp.), dawn redwoods (*Metasequoia glyptostroboides*), and bald cypress (*Taxodium distichum*) are three deciduous conifers. Ginkgo or maidenhair tree (*Ginkgo biloba*) is a deciduous conifer. Dwarf and low-growing conifers such as junipers are used as foundation or specimen plants and as ground covers.

Prune minimally. This applies to nearly all conifers. To keep bleeding to a minimum, prune as necessary from fall to midwinter. Cutting greens for holiday decorations fits into the proper pruning season nicely. For best results, when purchasing conifers that are to be grown as trees, look for plants with a single leader. Restrict pruning to removing dead, damaged, or wayward growth, and prune or train to maintain or replace the leader as necessary. When pruning or cutting greens, at least while plants are young, try to make pruning cuts that maintain a pyramidal shape. On both trees and shrubs, lower branches should extend farther than upper ones so that they receive adequate light; otherwise, the lower branches will gradually die off.

Consider compact forms. These are available for many evergreens and are the best choices for foundation plants, hedges, eye-catching specimens, and ground covers. Prune as necessary, using thinning cuts to remove branches.

Don't prune back hard. Whether you have trees or lower-growing shrubs, avoid cutting conifers back too hard, meaning don't cut into wood that does not have any needles on it. Most will not produce new shoots if they are cut back to bare or old

....

Weeping Trees

There are two types of weeping trees: ungrafted and grafted. Ungrafted weeping trees, including some forms of kousa dogwood (*Cornus kousa*), are generally created by staking a plant that has a weeping habit so that the bottom part of the plant is upright, but only because it is staked. (Some selections have weeping branch tips with an upright trunk.) The other type is more common and is created by grafting a weeping or prostrate form of a plant onto an upright trunk. Weeping cherries (*Prunus* spp.) and crab apples (*Malus* spp.) are two plants that are grafted to create a weeping tree.

On grafted specimens, use thinning cuts to remove any branches that begin to grow vertically. Most often, such branches arise from the upright trunk that the weeping, grafted portion of the tree is growing on. On ungrafted specimens, leave upright branches; with time, they eventually begin to weep.

For both types of weeping trees, remove lateral branches that appear on the trunk along with any suckers that arise around it. Also watch for congested growth and rubbing or crossing branches. Prune out the weaker of the two shoots.

....

wood. Instead of trying to chop a plant back to fit a spot where it is too large, consider replacing it with a new, more compact cultivar (nursery plant tags should provide height at maturity). Yews or taxus (*Taxus* spp.), Japanese cedar (*Cryptomeria japonica*), plumb yews (*Cephalotaxus* spp.), and young plants of bald cypress (*Taxodium distichum*) do tolerate being cut back to old wood.

PRUNING FRUIT TREES

Pruning and training fruit trees is something of a balancing act. It's essential that you guide growth so that branches are able to support the weight of a crop without cracking or breaking. It's also important to balance the speed of growth. Growth must be vigorous enough to produce flower buds and fruit annually, but growth that is too fast and too rank tends to be vegetative, meaning foliage but little or no flowers and fruit.

If you are planning an orchard, it's important to set aside the time necessary for annual pruning. Young trees need pruning and training, and mature trees need annual attention as well. Without regular pruning, the trees can quickly get out of hand. The good news is that overgrown trees can be renovated, especially if they have a sturdy central framework. (See Renovating Fruit Trees on page 72 for more information.)

There are many pruning styles for fruit trees, all of which balance these goals. Certain styles suit different types of trees — apple trees are typically pruned differently from peach trees, for example. Some styles require more maintenance than others. In addition, the majority of fruit trees are grafted plants:

the fruit-bearing scion is grafted onto a rootstock. Different rootstocks have different effects on growth. Many influence the tree's ultimate size at maturity, and dwarfing rootstocks are very popular. Rootstocks also can provide resistance to soil-borne diseases or nematodes, increase tolerance of wet soil, and affect hardiness. A plant's rootstock also affects pruning, because it influences the plant's overall vigor. In addition, grafted plants bear fruit sooner than ungrafted trees do.

The discussion that follows provides basic pruning information that will help you improve the health and structure of existing fruit trees. If you are planting new fruit trees or planning an orchard, you will need far more information on selecting rootstocks and pruning styles, among other topics. (See Suggested Reading for a list of references that provide extensive information on pruning and training fruit trees.)

Basic Pruning for Fruit Trees

There are several commonly used pruning and training styles for fruit trees that are relatively easy to implement and maintain. All fruit trees have branches that radiate from a central trunk. In general, treelike shapes are easier to create and require less pruning than two-dimensional pruning forms such as espalier, where branches are trained flat against a wall or on a fence or wires. (Espaliers and other two-dimensional forms are complicated, but they are space-efficient, quite handsome, and ideal for fitting fruit trees into small garden spaces.) A fruit tree's rootstock determines how easy it will be to train that particular tree into one of these forms.

(See Pruning Trees on page 44 for general guidelines for training a single-leader tree.)

Whatever form you select, aim for strong, broad branch angles, which are essential for supporting the weight of ripening fruit. When pruning, keep stems that are growing at angles of 60 to 90 degrees (that is, close to right angles) to the main trunk or branch. Young branches growing at narrower angles can be gently stretched down and held in place with tie-downs designed specifically for this purpose. The tie-downs are removed once the branch remains in the more horizontal position.

PRUNING, VIGOR, AND BEARING

Balancing growth across the entire tree is important. Use the basic rule presented in part 1: Prune weak branches hard to make them more vigorous, and prune vigorous branches lightly, if at all, to slow down growth. This principle is especially important with fruit trees because spindly, weak branches will not have the vigor needed to produce many flowers or fruit, while vigorous growth tends to be primarily vegetative.

Encouraging the production of wood that will flower and bear fruit is another important pruning goal. Apple and pear trees usually bear fruit on wood that is at least two and often three years old or older. New shoots arise one year, produce some flowers the second, then bear regularly after that. Many apple and pear cultivars produce their main crop on spurs, which are short, dense fruit-bearing stems that are at least three years old and bear annually. Since they are so important to production, spurs should be protected from damage. Bearing wood does need to be replaced or thinned out eventually so that it can be replaced by younger wood.

Peaches, nectarines, and sour cherries bear fruit on one-year-old wood, meaning growth from the previous season, so the main pruning goal should be the production of new shoots each season. Sweet cherries, plums, and apricots primarily bear their fruit on two-year-old wood, but they also produce some on one-year-old shoots as well.

MANY APPLES AND PEARS flower and fruit on spurs. Work carefully to avoid breaking the spurs, as they fruit for many years. To replace a spur once it begins to fruit less, select a strong shoot that is pointing toward the outside of the tree and cut off the spur that it is replacing.

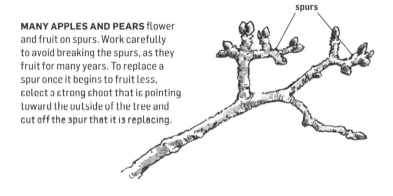

spurs

FRUIT TREE FORMS

Pyramid. The simplest form that suits apples, pears, cherries, and plums is a pyramid, which is essentially a single-leader tree with a straight central trunk and whorls of three or four branches radiating out in all directions like a Christmas tree, with the longest branches at the bottom to allow light to reach ripening fruit. The size of the tree and the spacing of the branches will depend on the dwarfing rootstock that was used. (This form is also suitable for pecan trees.) Branches should be as close to horizontal as possible, because horizontal growth favors flower and fruit production. The whorls of branches should be spaced out so that light and air can circulate within the plant for both ripening and disease prevention. The overall height of the tree and the number of branch whorls both depend on the rootstock.

fan

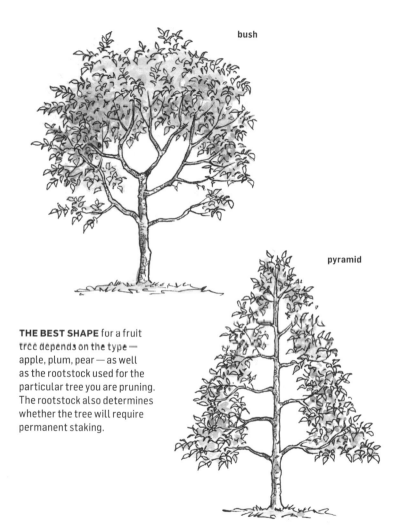

bush

pyramid

THE BEST SHAPE for a fruit tree depends on the type — apple, plum, pear — as well as the rootstock used for the particular tree you are pruning. The rootstock also determines whether the tree will require permanent staking.

Bush and half-standard. Another popular form that suits a wide variety of fruit trees is a short- to medium-length trunk (2½ to 3 feet) topped by a framework of branches that radiate in all directions, called a bush form. A half-standard tree is similar to a bush, but the trunk ranges from about 3½ to 4½ feet tall. Bush and half-standard trees are trained in much the same way that ornamental standard trees are trained. Here, too, the overall size of the resulting tree is determined by the rootstock.

Fan. Peaches, nectarines, and other stone fruits are often trained in a fan form. This form also is suitable for training figs. This form, too, has a short trunk, but the trunk is topped by two nearly horizontal main branches that are further divided into smaller branches.

TIMING

Proper timing of pruning is important for several reasons. Pruning invigorates plants that are pruned when they are dormant (from winter into early spring). Heavy dormant-season pruning can result in excessive vegetative growth, which does not produce flowers and fruit. Also, diseases, which can enter through pruning wounds, are more prevalent at certain times of the year. Stone fruits, including peaches, nectarines, plums, and cherries, are susceptible to fungal diseases that can enter through pruning wounds. Timing your pruning operations when the risk of disease is low helps control the spread of the disease. Check with your local Cooperative Extension Service for recommendations on when to prune your fruit trees, since timing varies according to climate.

In general, prune fruit trees as late as possible in winter. Here are three other useful guidelines for determining when to do dormant-season pruning:

- Prune apple trees first, followed by pears, then cherry, peach, and plum trees.
- In general, prune the latest-blooming trees first and the earliest-blooming last.
- If you have more than one fruit tree, prune the oldest tree first and the youngest tree last. That's because younger trees are more likely to be damaged by winter cold than older ones.

Apples and pears. Prune most apples from late winter to early spring, before flowering. Trees trained in espalier or in other forms where growth is closely controlled are pruned in summer to restrict growth.

Quince. Prune in winter.

Plums, sweet or sour cherries, peaches, nectarines, and apricots. Prune in spring as buds burst. Prune in summer where diseases and cankers that enter through pruning wounds are problematic. Remove diseased wood as soon as it appears, and prune out deadwood in summer or fall before the leaves fall.

Persimmons. See *Diospyros* spp. in the Tree-by-Tree Guide on page 56. Oriental persimmons (*D. kaki*) can be pruned and maintained as multi-stemmed trees. Plants require a strong framework and broad crotch angles, or they will break under fruit load.

Figs. Prune in spring after danger of extended frost has passed. They can be pruned as a low tree with 8 to 10 branches spaced out evenly. Remove crossing branches at the center of the plant and encourage an open center for adequate ripening.

Renovating Fruit Trees

Neglected fruit trees can be renovated and encouraged back into production. Spread out the renovation process over two or three years — more if the tree is badly overgrown — to minimize stress on the tree. When renovating, a good rule of thumb is to remove only 25 percent of the excess growth per year. Renovate trees at the same time of year they should be pruned. (See Timing on page 70.)

Year 1. As with all pruning projects, start by using thinning cuts to remove all broken, dead, or diseased branches. Next, eliminate rubbing and crossing growth. To open up the center of the tree to light and air, also remove some branches that cross the center of the tree or cause congested growth.

Year 2. Begin to shorten some of the branches that are too long by using thinning cuts to cut them back to a healthy replacement branch. Also remove succulent, upward-pointing watersprouts. Continue watching for these all summer long and clip them off whenever they appear.

Subsequent years. Once much of the excess growth has been removed and you have begun to shorten overly long branches, begin pruning annually to keep growth balanced throughout the tree and maintain fruit-bearing wood.

BEFORE PRUNING

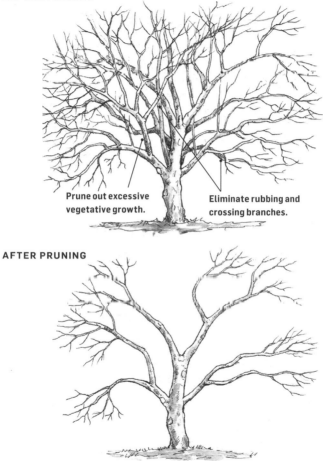

Prune out excessive vegetative growth.

Eliminate rubbing and crossing branches.

AFTER PRUNING

MAKE A PLAN when tackling an overgrown fruit tree. Eliminate deadwood and rubbing and crossing branches first; then tackle opening up the center of the plant and eliminating excessive vegetative growth over the course of several years.

PRUNING SHRUBS

EVERY SHRUB REQUIRES the same basic routine care: the removal of dead, diseased, and damaged wood, along with the elimination of rubbing and crossing branches. Some shrubs require little else in the way of regular attention, while others benefit from more specific trimming and shaping. The best approach not only varies according to species but also depends on the role a particular shrub plays in the landscape. Is it primarily grown for abundant flowers, showy foliage, colorful stems, or privacy?

For shrubs grown for flowers, timing is especially important, since some plants produce flower buds on **new wood** and others on **old wood**. If you are not sure of the identity of the shrub, the following general rules provide a helpful guideline:

Shrubs with spring and early summer flowers. Prune these shrubs immediately after the flowers fade, since these generally bloom on old wood (growth produced the previous growing season).

Shrubs with midsummer to fall flowers. Prune in late winter or early spring, since these generally bloom on new wood (wood produced during the current season).

Keep in mind that some shrubs bloom on both new and old wood. These can be pruned on either schedule. Minimal pruning will produce the most flowers.

Pruning for Privacy

For shrubs used in hedges, foundation plantings, and privacy screens, ideally you use thinning cuts to establish the overall shape of the plant and heading cuts to encourage branching and bushy growth toward branch tips. Another option is to combine taller, vase-shaped shrubs with lower-growing mounding to pyramidal ones to create a thick screen. Always aim to maintain a roughly pyramidal shape, with lower branches that reach out farther than upper ones. This ensures that light reaches the lower branches so that leaves toward the bottom of the plant remain thick and the plant provides the privacy you are looking for.

For formal hedges and foundation plants that are sculpted into mounds or rectangles, shearing is popular. This is a high-maintenance choice, since shearing essentially consists of hundreds of heading cuts, each of which spurs new growth. Sheared hedges need pruning twice a year: once during winter and again in midsummer. Shearing also means that the individual cuts are not made properly, because the shears clip along the sides of the plant without regard to the location of buds on individual stems. Sheared hedges are effective privacy screens and are especially useful where space is an issue. Be sure to shape shrubs used in this manner so that they are wider at the bottom than the top; this allows light to reach the lower leaves.

Basic Pruning Approaches for Shrubs

Keep in mind that, if necessary, nearly any shrub can be successfully pruned from late winter into early spring, although this will mean sacrificing flowers for a season on many species. To determine what approach will be most beneficial for a particular shrub, read the pruning recommendations for that species included in the Shrub-by-Shrub Pruning Guide beginning on page 82. Use that information together with the pruning approaches described here. Always start by removing any dead or diseased growth.

BASIC ANNUAL PRUNING

Many shrubs, both deciduous and evergreen, need little more than basic annual pruning. Since few flower buds are removed, this approach is suitable for shrubs that bloom on new wood (growth produced in the current growing season) as well as old wood (growth produced the previous year).

How: Use thinning cuts to remove dead or diseased growth. Eliminate rubbing or crossing branches by eliminating the weaker of the two branches. Prune out congested growth to create a pleasing, balanced shape; promote healthy air circulation; and highlight the natural shape of the plant. Also use thinning cuts to shorten any overly long shoots or wayward growth by cutting them back to another branch. Use heading cuts, if necessary, to encourage branching and create denser growth.

When: Prune in late winter or early spring, unless otherwise noted in the Shrub-by-Shrub Pruning Guide on page 82.

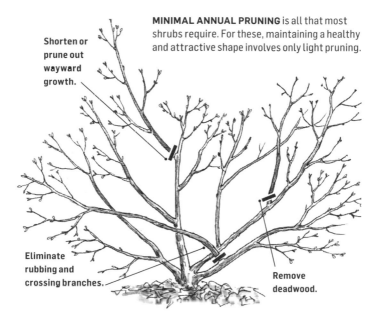

Shorten or prune out wayward growth.

MINIMAL ANNUAL PRUNING is all that most shrubs require. For these, maintaining a healthy and attractive shape involves only light pruning.

Eliminate rubbing and crossing branches.

Remove deadwood.

ANNUAL PRUNING FOR FLOWERING EVERGREENS

This approach is suitable for shaping evergreen shrubs that require minimal pruning and flower from late winter to early summer. Typically, plants that bloom this time of year produce flowers on old wood (growth produced the previous growing season).

How: Use thinning cuts to remove dead and diseased wood as well as crossing, rubbing, or congested branches to create a pleasing, balanced shape and promote healthy growth. Prune so that lower branches reach out farther than upper ones. This ensures that the lower leaves receive light and that the lower branches remain healthy. Trim back any overly long shoots or wayward growth as necessary. Always cut just above a shoot or a bud that is pointing in the direction you want the growth to go. Remove spent flowers if desired.

When: Prune in late spring or early summer, as soon as flowers fade, unless otherwise noted in the Shrub-by-Shrub Pruning Guide on page 82.

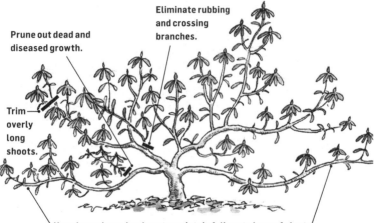

Eliminate rubbing and crossing branches.

Prune out dead and diseased growth.

Trim overly long shoots.

Keep lower branches long to maintain foliage to base of plant.

FLOWERING EVERGREENS generally require minimal pruning. Keep an eye out for dead and diseased wood, and also eliminate rubbing and crossing branches as well as overly congested growth.

REGULAR RENEWAL PRUNING

Renewal pruning is suitable for shrubs that produce flower buds on old wood (growth produced the previous year) and that bloom best on vigorous, younger wood. Once plants are established and growing strongly, remove some of the older shoots annually to promote the formation of new growth.

How: Each year, start by removing one-quarter to one-third of the oldest stems. Cut stems to be removed back to the base of the plant or to a strong, well-placed side shoot. The best

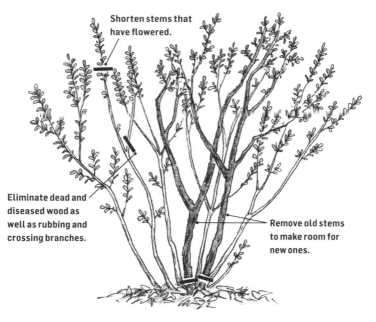

Shorten stems that have flowered.

Eliminate dead and diseased wood as well as rubbing and crossing branches.

Remove old stems to make room for new ones.

REGULAR RENEWAL PRUNING ensures a continuing supply of vigorous new wood, removing a portion of the older stems each year.

stems to remove are ones that crowd the center of the plant or affect its overall symmetry. Stem removal also opens up the center of the plant to improve air circulation. Once these stems have been removed, shape the rest of the plant by following the directions provided in Basic Annual Pruning on page 76. If desired, use heading cuts to remove spent flowers. Always cut back to just above a healthy, vigorous bud that is pointing in the direction you want the growth to go.

When: Each year immediately after flowers fade.

FRAMEWORK PRUNING

Many shrubs that flower from mid- to late summer benefit from hard annual pruning, which encourages good flower production and keeps the branches from getting large and rangy. In most cases, framework pruning is used on deciduous shrubs that produce flowers on new wood (growth produced during the current season). It is also used on plants grown for colorful winter stems, because younger stems typically exhibit the best color. (However, regular renewal pruning, described on page 79, can also be used to maintain colorful stems and is less stressful for the plant.) Finally, although framework pruning eliminates flowers on plants that set buds on old wood, it also is used to encourage extra-large, colorful foliage on some species.

How: As buds begin to swell in early spring, cut stems back to within 1 or 2 feet of the ground to create a low framework of woody growth. Look for healthy, swollen buds on the woody stems at the base of the plant. Leave at least two to three buds on each stem. Depending on the species and the vigor of the plant, leave more healthy buds on each stem. For a hard renovation, cut stems nearly to the ground. When cutting a shrub to the ground, watch for buds to break; then remove any growth above these new shoots using thinning cuts. Cut the stems of suckering shrubs close to the base of the plant. Since this technique removes healthy growth and will stress the plants, after pruning, spread a layer of compost or well-rotted manure topped by mulch.

When: Annually in early spring, once buds begin to swell.

Leave two to three healthy buds on each stem.

FRAMEWORK PRUNING is used on shrubs that bloom from midsummer to fall. Cutting them back hard in early spring promotes flowers later in the season.

Shrub-by-Shrub Pruning Guide

The plant list below provides pruning recommendations for a wide variety of popular species. Use it to determine the best techniques to keep your plants healthy and vigorous. Since proper timing is important for flowering shrubs, the list indicates when to prune as well as the best technique to use. Some species listed are considered invasive, meaning they are non-native plants that reproduce rapidly and have escaped cultivation. Since these plants are still commonly grown and sold, they are included here because they also require pruning. Consider replacing invasives with less problematic species by consulting your local Cooperative Extension office or a high-quality local nursery or garden center.

Abelia spp. (abelias). Use basic annual pruning (page 76) to manage deciduous species; use annual pruning for flowering evergreens (page 77) for evergreen species. On established plants, use regular renewal pruning (page 79). Plants can be renovated by cutting all stems to the ground in early spring.

Abeliophyllum distichum (white forsythia). Use regular renewal pruning (page 79) immediately after flowering in spring. Use thinning cuts to remove stems, cutting back to stems close to the base of the plant. This encourages younger wood, which blooms best. Plants can be renovated using framework pruning (page 80) immediately after flowers fade in spring.

Aesculus parviflora (bottlebrush buckeye). Prune minimally. Use basic annual pruning (page 76).

Amelanchier spp. (serviceberries). Prune minimally. Use basic annual pruning (page 76) either in winter or immediately after flowering in spring. Thin congested clumps using regular renewal pruning (page 79) every two or three years, removing up to one-third of the stems.

Aronia **spp. (chokeberries).** Use basic annual pruning (page 76), if necessary. Plants bear flowers on old wood (growth produced the previous year) and can be pruned either in winter, which removes some flower buds, or immediately after flowering in summer, which prevents berry production. Once plants are established, begin regular renewal pruning (page 79), removing up to one-third of the oldest stems. If necessary, restrict the size of the clump by removing suckers or digging and transplanting them.

Aucuba japonica **(Japanese aucuba).** Use basic annual pruning (page 76). To encourage bushy growth, use heading cuts to cut shoots back by about one-third in spring. To renew overgrown plants or reshape plants that have lost leaves at the base, use regular renewal pruning (page 79). Over several years, remove up to one-third of the stems annually.

Bamboos. Individual stems do not respond to conventional pruning. Cut canes at the base of the plant to open up stands to light and air. Most bamboos can be renovated by cutting all canes to the ground. Many species of bamboo are considered invasive.

Berberis **(barberries).** Use basic annual pruning (page 76) to manage deciduous species; use annual pruning for flowering evergreens (page 77) for evergreen species. Keep plants vigorous by using regular renewal pruning (page 79). For more drastic renovation, use framework pruning (page 80) in late spring. Japanese barberry (*B. thunbergii*) is invasive.

Buddleja **spp. (butterfly bushes).** Use framework pruning (page 80) for common butterfly bush (*B. davidii*); regular renewal pruning (page 79) on alternate-leaved butterfly bush (*B. alternifolia*). Common butterfly bush (*B. davidii*) is invasive.

Buxus **spp. (boxwoods).** Prune boxwoods in mid- to late summer using annual pruning for flowering evergreens (page 77) to highlight their natural shape. Maintaining their natural shape minimizes the need to prune. Boxwoods tolerate hard renovation pruning but take several years to recover. To renovate, use framework pruning (page 80) in late spring.

Callicarpa **spp. (beautyberries).** Use regular renewal pruning (page 79) or framework pruning (page 80) in early spring.

Calluna **spp. (heathers).** Cut stems back in spring to within ½ inch of the previous season's growth.

Calycanthus floridus **(sweet shrub, Carolina allspice).** Use basic annual pruning (page 76). Prune immediately after flowering if necessary. Cut back branch tips to shape plant and encourage bushy growth. Sweet shrubs can be cut back hard using framework pruning (page 80) if they become too large. Plants can spread by suckering; if desired, remove suckers below ground to reduce spread.

Camellia **spp. (camellias).** Use annual pruning for flowering evergreens (page 77) to shape plants, pruning Japanese camellias (*C. japonica*) in spring immediately after flowering. Prune fall-blooming *C. sasanqua* cultivars in spring before growth begins. Use thinning cuts to cut back overly long branches and reshape plants so that they are widest at the bottom. This prevents leaf loss at the bottom of the plant due to shading. Both

Pruning Brambles

Blackberries, raspberries, loganberries, and other similar crops can seem like vines because their long canes can become so unruly. The best bramble crops are borne on one-year-old canes. The goal of pruning is to remove canes that have already fruited to make room for new, more vigorous growth. For best fruit production, they require training as well as pruning. (See Suggested Reading for more complete information on training systems.) The simplest way to manage the thorny canes, both for pruning and for harvesting, is to use a system that separates the fruit-producing canes from the new ones that arise from the base of the plant each year and bear next year's fruit.

Pruning is fairly simple: In spring of the first year, cut back the canes on newly planted brambles so they are 8 to 12 inches tall. This encourages new canes to form. Remove the original cane in midsummer. In fall, remove canes that have flowered and borne fruit by cutting them back to the base of the plant. In late winter or early spring, use heading cuts to shorten each of the new canes by about 6 inches. Also remove any suckers or canes that appear near the plants, because brambles quickly form a thicket, making caring for the thorny plants difficult.

For autumn-bearing raspberries, do not remove fruited canes in fall. Instead, cut all canes to the ground in late winter. The fruit is borne on the new canes produced in the current year.

types tolerate hard pruning; use framework pruning (page 80) to renovate during the seasons mentioned above.

Caryopteris × *clandonensis* (bluebeard). Cut back plants in mid- to late spring once buds begin to swell. Use framework pruning (page 80); however, plants generally will not sprout from old wood, so leave at least 1 to 2 inches of new wood (wood produced the previous season) on the plant. To renovate an overgrown plant, cut back hard, but locate live, healthy buds on the plant and leave at least two or three of them on each stem.

Ceanothus spp. (New Jersey tea, California lilac). Use annual pruning for flowering evergreens (page 77) for evergreen species (primarily tender shrubs), pruning after flowers fade. Use framework pruning (page 80) in early spring for deciduous species, including New Jersey tea (*C. americanus*).

Chaenomeles spp. (flowering quinces). Prune minimally. Use regular renewal pruning (page 79) after flowering from late spring to early summer. To maximize flowering, use heading cuts to shorten all side shoots back to two or three leaves.

Chimonanthus (wintersweet). Prune minimally. Use regular renewal pruning (page 79).

Clethra spp. (clethra, sweet pepperbush). Use regular renewal pruning (page 79) in winter once plants are established.

Cornus spp. (dogwoods). Minimal pruning is best for dogwoods, both shrubs and trees. Use basic annual pruning (page 76) for most species. For species grown for colorful stems (*C. alba, C. sanguinea, C. stolonifera*), use framework pruning (page 80) or regular renewal pruning (page 79).

Corylopsis spp. (winter hazels). Prune minimally. Use basic annual pruning (page 76), if necessary, immediately after flowering.

Corylus spp. (filberts, hazels). Use basic annual pruning (page 76) as needed. Remove suckers that arise, especially from the roots of grafted specimens. On fully established plants, remove occasional older stems using regular renewal pruning (page 79).

Cotinus spp. (smoke trees). For most plants, prune in early spring before growth begins using basic annual pruning (page 76). To produce plants that highlight large, showy foliage, use framework pruning (page 80) before growth begins; this prevents flowering. When framework pruning, only cut stems back by about three-quarters and be sure to leave two or more healthy buds on each branch to ensure vigorous regrowth.

Cotoneaster spp. (cotoneasters). Prune from late winter to early spring, using basic annual pruning (page 76) for deciduous species; use annual pruning for flowering evergreens (page 77) for evergreen species. Plants can be cut back hard or renovated by cutting branches close to the ground.

Cytisus spp. (brooms). Use basic annual pruning (page 76) for most species, and prune immediately after flowering, which ranges from early to late summer. Prune *C. nigricans* in late winter or early spring.

Daphne spp. (daphnes). Prune as little as possible, removing only dead or diseased growth.

Deutzia spp. (deutzias). Prune after flowers fade in late spring. Use regular renewal pruning (page 79), since old wood does not bloom as well as young wood does. To ensure a supply of young, new wood, cut up to one-third of the oldest stems to the ground and use thinning cuts to clip out older wood on other stems, cutting to just above new side shoots.

Diervilla spp. (bush honeysuckles). Use framework pruning (page 80) annually in early spring. Cut plants back hard, leaving only two or three buds on each stem.

Elaeagnus spp. (elaegnus). Prune minimally. Use basic annual pruning (page 76) on deciduous species; use annual pruning for flowering evergreens (page 77) for evergreen species. Prune in mid- to late summer, which is immediately after flowering for most common species. Remove reverted growth on variegated plants. Elaeagnus can be renovated by cutting back to old wood. Autumn olive (*E. umbellata*) and Russian-olive (*E. angustifolia*) are invasive.

Erica spp. (heaths, heathers). In spring, cut stems back immediately after flowering to within ½ inch of the previous season's growth.

Euonymus spp. (euonymus). Prune from late winter to early spring using basic annual pruning (page 76) for deciduous species; use annual pruning for flowering evergreens (page 77) for evergreen species. Remove any all-green reverted growth that appears on variegated selections. Wintercreeper (*E. fortunei*) is invasive.

Forsythia spp. (forsythias). Prune immediately after flowering using regular renewal pruning (page 79). Cut one-third to one-half of the oldest woody stems back to the ground or use thinning cuts to cut back to stems close to the base of the plant. This encourages younger wood, which blooms best. For hard renovation, cut the entire plant to the ground in winter. This eliminates the next season's flowers, but plants recover quickly.

Fothergilla spp. (fothergillas). Prune minimally. Use basic annual pruning (page 76) if necessary.

Hamamelis spp. (witch hazels). Prune minimally. Prune in early spring after flowering but before the leaves emerge using basic annual pruning (page 76). Remove any suckers that grow from the rootstock on grafted plants.

Hibiscus spp. (hibiscus, rose of Sharon). Prune in late spring using basic annual pruning (page 76) for deciduous species; use annual pruning for flowering evergreens (page 77) for evergreen species. Use heading cuts to shorten branches and encourage bushier growth. To renovate hibiscus or correct lopsided growth, use thinning cuts to cut older branches back to a branch closer to the base of the plant or remove them by cutting to the ground. Then cut back branches that remain on the plant hard to encourage branching and bushy growth.

Hydrangea spp. (hydrangeas). Prune most hydrangeas in early spring using basic annual pruning (page 76). Wild hydrangea (*H. arborescens*) and panicle or peegee hydrangea (*H. paniculata*) bloom on new wood (wood produced during the current season) and can be pruned in early spring using framework pruning (page 80). Wild hydrangea can be cut to the ground in spring. Panicle hydrangea can be left unpruned or cut to a framework as short as 1 to 2 feet or as tall as 6 to 10 feet. Panicle hydrangeas also can be trained as small trees. Prune bigleaf hydrangeas (*H. macrophylla*) in mid-spring. First remove flowers from the previous year. On established plants, use regular renewal pruning (page 79) to remove some of the older stems. To shape plants and encourage vigorous new growth that will produce flowers, use heading cuts to shorten stems, cutting just above healthy buds. New reblooming bigleaf hydrangeas bloom on both old and new wood, and they can be shaped or pruned anytime during the year without eliminating all of that year's blooms. Most hydrangeas can be renovated using framework pruning (page 80) in spring.

Hypericum spp. (St. John's worts). Prune most St. John's worts in spring. Use basic annual pruning (page 76) for deciduous species; use annual pruning for flowering evergreens (page 77) for evergreen species. Cut Aaron's beard (*H. calycinum*) to the ground in early spring. Most St. John's worts can be renovated by cutting them to the ground in spring.

Ilex spp. (hollies). Most shrubby hollies need minimal pruning to look their best. Use basic annual pruning (page 76) in spring to shape as necessary. Keep plants, especially evergreens, wider at the base so that lower leaves are not shaded. Established plants can be shaped in summer. Pruning to collect branches for holiday decorations in early winter is fine as well. *See also: Ilex opaca* (page 58).

Itea spp. (sweetspires). For deciduous species, including *I. virginica*, use regular renewal pruning (page 79) in winter. Use annual pruning for flowering evergreens (page 77) for evergreen species.

Kalmia spp. (mountain laurels). Prune immediately after flowering using annual pruning for flowering evergreens (page 77). Overgrown plants can be renovated by cutting back the branches nearly to the ground in spring. This is best done over three or more seasons, and plants take several years to recover.

Kerria japonica (kerria). Prune in late spring immediately after flowering using regular renewal pruning (page 79). Dig up suckers, as necessary, to reduce spreading. Plants can be renovated by cutting all stems to the ground in spring.

Kolkwitzia amabilis (beautybush). Prune immediately after flowering in midsummer using regular renewal pruning (page 79).

Lavandula spp. (lavender). Where winters are cold, prune in spring, since growth left on the plant helps protect buds from cold. Deadheading, or removing flower stems only, is fine in fall. In warm climates, where lavenders are completely hardy, prune in fall. To prune, cut stems back to within $1/2$ inch of the previous season's growth. Plants generally do not resprout from old wood.

Laurus nobilis (bay laurel). Prune in late winter to early spring using regular renewal pruning (page 79). Prune to shape plants as needed in summer as well.

Ligustrum spp. (privets). Prune from late winter to early spring using basic annual pruning (page 76). Prune privets grown as hedges once or twice, as needed, in summer. Old privets can be cut back hard using framework pruning (page 80) for renovation. Most species are invasive.

Lonicera spp. (honeysuckles). Prune in spring immediately after flowering using regular renewal pruning (page 79). Plants in hedges and screen plantings can be pruned as needed during summer. Most shrubby honeysuckles are invasive.

Magnolia spp. (magnolias). These generally are best with minimal pruning. Prune in midsummer using basic annual pruning (page 76) for deciduous species and annual pruning for flowering evergreens (page 77) for evergreen species. *See also: Magnolia* spp. on page 58.

Mahonia spp. (mahonias, grapehollies). Most require minimal pruning. Use annual pruning for flowering evergreens (page 77) after flowering in spring. Cut back old or damaged stems to the base of the plant, and remove suckers on the outside of the clumps if plants spread too far. Ground-cover types can be sheared to the ground every two or three years.

Morella spp. (formerly *Myrica* spp.; bayberries). Prune minimally. Use basic annual pruning (page 76) as necessary.

Nandina domestica (nandina, heavenly bamboo). Prune minimally. Use annual pruning for flowering evergreens (page 77) in spring. Remove old or overgrown stems as necessary, to keep the plants attractive, by cutting them to the ground. Invasive.

Nerium oleander (oleander). Plants require little pruning. Prune from late summer to fall after flowering using annual pruning for flowering evergreens (page 77). Oleanders can tolerate hard pruning, but they will take several years to recover. The sap is poisonous, so wear gloves and avoid contact.

Osmanthus spp. (osmanthus). Use annual pruning for flowering evergreens (page 77). Prune early-blooming species in mid- to late spring immediately after flowering. Prune late-blooming species in early spring. These require minimal pruning, but they can withstand hard pruning and being cut back into old wood.

Paeonia spp. (tree peonies). Deadhead tree peonies immediately after flowering in spring using basic annual pruning (page 76). For species with ornamental seeds, deadhead in fall. Minimal pruning is best, but on older plants occasionally cut an older stem to the ground to encourage new growth.

Perovskia atriplicifolia (Russian sage). Prune in spring as buds begin to swell using framework pruning (page 80).

Philadelphus spp. (mock oranges). Prune in late summer immediately after flowering using regular renewal pruning (page 79). On overgrown plants that need renovation, cut back hard in late winter or early spring using framework pruning (page 80).

Photinia spp. (photinias). These typically need only basic annual pruning (page 76) in spring. When grown as hedges, shape in spring and summer. Renovate plants if necessary by cutting them back hard. They will resprout from old wood.

Physocarpus spp. (ninebarks). Use basic annual pruning (page 76) to shape plants as necessary. Once they are established, begin using regular renewal pruning (page 79) immediately after flowering.

Pieris spp. (pieris). Shape plants as necessary using annual pruning for flowering evergreens (page 77). They can be renovated, if necessary, by cutting back hard into old wood using framework pruning (page 80).

Prunus spp. (cherries, cherry laurels, flowering almond). Prune most deciduous shrubs from late winter to early spring using basic annual pruning (page 76). Cut back dwarf flowering almonds (*P. glandulosa* and *P. triloba*) hard using framework pruning (page 80) immediately after flowering. Use annual pruning for flowering evergreens (page 77) for evergreen shrubs immediately after flowering. Prune species grown only for foliage in mid- to late spring.

Pyracantha spp. (firethorns). Prune in late winter to early spring using basic annual pruning (page 76). Trim hedges in spring or early summer.

Rhododendron spp. (rhododendrons and azaleas). Prune in spring or early summer, immediately after flowering, using basic annual pruning (page 76) for deciduous azaleas; use annual pruning for flowering evergreens (page 77) for evergreen azaleas and rhododendrons.

Rhus spp. (sumacs). Prune most sumacs using basic annual pruning (page 76). Use framework pruning (page 80) in early spring for staghorn sumac (*R. typhina*). Remove unwanted suckers when they appear.

Ribes spp. (currants and gooseberries). Use regular renewal pruning (page 79) in mid- to late spring, immediately after flowering. Renovate plants by cutting stems to the ground in spring. For best fruit production, remove branches that cross or crowd the center of the bush so that light and air can circulate. Your goal should be an upright framework of main branches that radiate out. Use heading cuts to remove the tip of each framework branch; then use heading cuts to shorten all side branches that grow off the main framework branches to one bud. Remove branches that arise too close to the ground. Occasionally remove an older branch, and select a new, younger branch to replace it. If growth is very vigorous, prune again in midsummer to cut back side shoots to five leaves.

Rosmarinus officinalis (rosemary). Prune in late spring using annual pruning for flowering evergreens (page 77).

Salix spp. (willows). Use basic annual pruning (page 76) from late winter to early spring. For species grown for colorful stems, cut plants back using framework pruning (page 80) every one to three years. Many species are invasive.

Sambucus spp. (elderberries, elders). Use framework pruning (page 80) in early spring for plants grown primarily for their showy foliage. Otherwise, use basic annual pruning (page 76). Elderberries can be cut back hard using framework pruning for renovation or to restrict size.

Salvia spp. (sages, salvias). Trim plants in spring using annual pruning for flowering evergreens (page 77).

Santolina spp. (santolinas, lavender cottons). Cut back stems to within $1/2$ inch of the previous season's growth in spring. Remove spent flowers in fall. Young, vigorous plants resprout from old wood, so cut them back hard every few years to keep them compact.

Skimmia japonica (skimmia). Prune minimally. Use annual pruning for flowering evergreens (page 77) if necessary.

Spiraea spp. (spiraeas). Prune summer-blooming species, including Japanese spirea (*S. japonica*), using framework pruning (page 80) in spring. Prune other spireas immediately after flowering using regular renewal pruning (page 79). Japanese spirea (*S. japonica*) is invasive.

Symphoricarpos spp. (snowberries). Prune in early spring using regular renewal pruning (page 79). Plants can be renovated by cutting all stems to the ground or by cutting back hard using framework pruning (page 80).

Syringa spp. (lilacs). Prune in early summer, immediately after the flowers have faded. Common lilac (*S. vulgaris*) can be renovated by cutting back stems to within 1 or 2 feet of the ground using framework pruning (page 80). Spreading the renovation over several seasons is best. Thin growth that sprouts after this process. Remove suckers when they appear, especially on grafted specimens.

Tamarix spp. (tamarisks). Prune spring-blooming species annually immediately after flowering using regular renewal pruning (page 79). Prune species that bloom in late summer using framework pruning (page 80). Tamarisks are invasive.

Vaccinium spp. (blueberries, huckleberries). Prune in late winter or early spring using basic annual pruning (page 76). Once plants are well established, use regular renewal pruning (page 79) to ensure a supply of young wood, which bears more heavily than old wood. Cut stems to be removed all the way to the ground or use a thinning cut to remove a healthy young shoot that is pointing in the direction you want growth to go.

Viburnum spp. (viburnums). Prune viburnums immediately after flowering in early to midsummer using basic annual pruning (page 76). Most plants require minimal pruning. Remove upright watersprouts on doublefile viburnum (*V. plicatum* var. *tomentosum*). European cranberrybush viburnum (*V. opulus*) is invasive.

Vitex spp. (chaste trees). Use framework pruning (page 80) in spring.

Weigela spp. (weigelas). Prune in early summer immediately after flowering using regular renewal pruning (page 79). Weigelas can be renovated by cutting all stems to the ground in early spring.

Zenobia pulverulenta (zenobia). Prune in midsummer using regular renewal pruning (page 79). Plants can be renovated using framework pruning (page 80) in spring.

PRUNING ROSES

PROPER PRUNING NOT ONLY KEEPS ROSES HEALTHY and vigorous but also promotes maximum bloom. Insufficient pruning reduces flower size, quantity, and quality. For climbing and rambling roses, training also plays a role; although horizontal training is not always practical, canes bloom best when trained this way.

The genus *Rosa*, to which all roses belong, contains about 150 species of deciduous and evergreen roses that have been hybridized extensively to produce a dizzying array of plant types and literally thousands of cultivars. While rose experts and collectors will want to use more detailed pruning references, the discussion here provides the basic information most gardeners need to keep their plants pruned, attractive, and blooming.

Rose Group Pruning Guide

Roses are shrubs, and their pruning requirements are quite similar. When you start pruning a rosebush, first remove dead, diseased, or damaged wood. Healthy young canes are green, while dead ones are brown and dry. Diseased canes are also discolored. Also eliminate any rubbing and crossing branches. On grafted roses, eliminate suckers that have arisen from the rootstock, below the graft union. Use thinning cuts to remove spindly stems, which will not bloom; on most roses, this means stems that are thinner than a pencil. By far, the easiest roses to maintain are the new hybrid shrub roses, which can be maintained using regular renewal pruning (page 79).

The best season for pruning roses varies depending on your climate. In colder areas, where winter damage is common, wait until early spring to prune. This makes it possible to see healthy buds that are swelling and identify cold-damaged growth. Elsewhere, prune in late winter.

Hybrid tea, grandiflora, and hybrid perpetual roses. Prune in late winter or early spring. On established roses, identify three to five healthy stems to form the framework of the plant, and cut off the rest at the base of the plant. Aim to remove stems toward the center of the plant to reduce congestion and improve air circulation. Remember: **Hard pruning** is essential for good bloom. In most areas, cut back the main framework stems to a height of 8 to 12 inches. In climates where roses bloom for much of the

Rose-Cutting Basics

- Always make cuts that are no more than ¼ inch above an outward-facing bud. Use sharp hand pruners to avoid leaving damaged or bruised wood above the bud. As with all proper heading cuts, do not leave a stub. Slant each cut away from the bud, so that water does not collect against it.

- To direct growth outward and prevent congested growth at the center of the plant, cut above buds that face toward the outside of the bush.

- Make all cuts into healthy wood. After each cut, look for white pith at the center of the cane. Brown or discolored pith indicates unhealthy wood, so cut the cane back farther until the pith is white.

year, leave the framework branches longer — 18 to 24 inches. Cut back side shoots to two or three buds or to a length of 4 to 6 inches. Always cut above outward-facing buds. Once plants are established, begin renewal pruning by cutting one or two of the oldest main framework branches (up to one-third of the total main canes) to the base of the plant annually. Select healthy, new stems to replace them. Wait to begin renewal pruning on newly planted roses until plants are established.

Floribunda, miniature, and polyantha roses. Prune as for hybrid tea, grandiflora, and hybrid perpetual roses, above, but on floribundas, cut back stems to about 18 inches. Cut back side stems to two or three buds or to a length of 4 to 6 inches

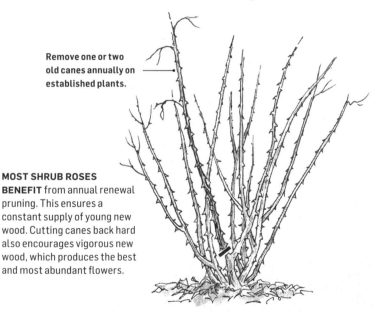

Remove one or two old canes annually on established plants.

MOST SHRUB ROSES BENEFIT from annual renewal pruning. This ensures a constant supply of young new wood. Cutting canes back hard also encourages vigorous new wood, which produces the best and most abundant flowers.

on most plants. On dwarf and miniature cultivars, cut back by one-third to one-half.

Climbing and rambling roses. Prune climbing roses from winter to early spring, depending on where you live. Cut back main shoots to fit the trellis or other support, and shorten side shoots by about two-thirds or to three or four buds. Cut back old stems that no longer bloom well to a vigorous shoot. Once plants are established, begin renewal pruning: Each year, cut back one or two of the oldest canes to within 1 to 1½ feet of the ground. Select a young, healthy cane(s) to replace it. Prune rambling roses like climbing roses, but prune them immediately after flowering in midsummer. Remove up to one-third of

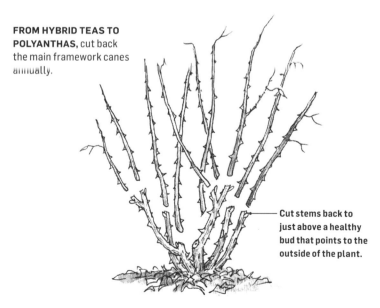

FROM HYBRID TEAS TO POLYANTHAS, cut back the main framework canes annually.

Cut stems back to just above a healthy bud that points to the outside of the plant.

the older stems annually on established plants. Cut out canes in sections, since pulling long canes through the plant will damage it. For both climbing and rambling roses, training the shoots horizontally produces the most flowers.

Shrub roses and species roses. In summer, immediately after the main flush of flowers, use thinning cuts to lightly prune main stems to shape and reduce congestion, cutting them back by up to about one-third. Cut back side shoots by one-half to two-thirds. These do not require the hard framework pruning that hybrid teas and grandifloras require for good bloom. Once plants are established, begin to renewal-prune: Cut one or two of the oldest main framework branches (up to one-third of the total main canes) to the base of the plant annually. Select healthy, new stems to replace them. For reblooming shrub and species roses, prune, as above, in late winter or early spring. For alba, centifolia, damask, moss, eglanteria, gallica, and hybrid spinosissima roses, prune as above, but cut back main framework canes only by one-quarter to one-third and shorten side shoots by two-thirds. When renewing plants, remove only a quarter of the main canes annually, and cut back the rest by one-third. For gallica roses, remove only one to two stems every two or three years.

PRUNING VINES

WHILE THE BASIC PRUNING PRINCIPLES APPLY to vines just as they do to shrubs and trees, vines can seem overwhelming simply because their stems are long, intertwined, and unruly. The good news is that many vines grow just fine with minimal attention. While most can be pruned "in place," meaning while still attached to their support, another option is to detach the vine from the trellis or other support, lay it on the ground, and prune it there before standing it up and reattaching it.

Training Vines

Newly planted vines need special pruning attention for the first few seasons. During this period, select several strong, vigorous framework stems that will cover the support evenly. Plant vines about a foot away from supports, and use stakes or string to direct shoots onto the support itself. (Vines also can be trained and maintained to cover walls and low obstacles such as rock piles.) Shorten branches to encourage branching and bushy growth. Remove any spindly stems in order to direct plant growth into the most vigorous ones. Reposition healthy stems that are growing in the wrong direction, and tie them in place.

Keep in mind that the amount of pruning a vine requires only partly depends on the species in question. The size of the vine's trellis or other support is also a factor. Some vines are simply larger and more vigorous than others. A large vine trained onto a too-small trellis needs considerably more pruning than the same species growing on a substantial support. Also, for large supports where pruning promises to be difficult, vines that require minimal pruning are best, simply because they need less attention.

Deadheading, or removing spent blooms, is entirely optional. While it will extend the bloom season of some vines, deadheading is not necessary and quite often completely impractical because much of the plant may not be accessible. Do not remove spent flowers if a vine is grown for its fruit, whether edible or ornamental.

As a general rule, prune deciduous vines during the dormant season. Evergreen vines are most often pruned in spring because new growth quickly covers up the pruned branch tips. Whether or not a vine is grown for its flowers also affects when it should be pruned. Use the Vine-by-Vine Pruning Guide (page 109) together with the two basic pruning strategies described below to determine the best approach for the vines in your garden.

Basic Vine Pruning

This approach is suitable for a great many vines, especially large, vigorous ones. Use it to chop back a climber to fit a trellis or other support as well as to keep a large vine shapely and in check. Prune annually or whenever a vine outgrows its space or support. Summer pruning can help keep a plant's growth under control. Use the Vine-by-Vine Pruning Guide beginning on page 109 to determine the best time to prune.

For vigorous vines that have completely outgrown their corner of the garden, have considerable amounts of old and declining growth, or have stopped flowering, renovation may be an option. (See box below for more information.)

Renovation

Older vines gradually lose vigor and benefit from renovation pruning. Vines can be renovated in two ways: either cut the entire plant to the ground and then select and train new main shoots that appear, or renovate gradually over several years. To spread out the renovation process, remove one or two declining stems annually by cutting them off at the base of the plant. Select new, vigorous stems to train in their place. Either way, renovate vines when they are dormant, from winter to early spring.

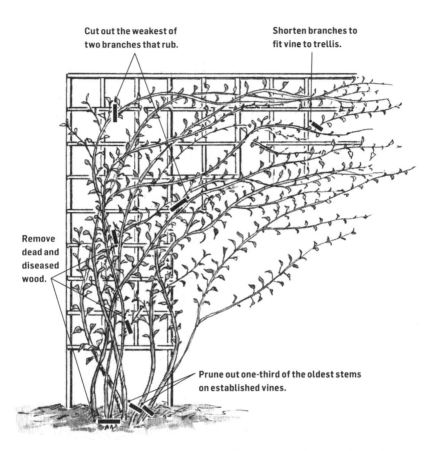

Cut out the weakest of two branches that rub.

Shorten branches to fit vine to trellis.

Remove dead and diseased wood.

Prune out one-third of the oldest stems on established vines.

LARGE, VIGOROUS VINES can be especially difficult to prune. Take your time and step back frequently to assess the plant and your progress.

How: As with any pruning operation, start by removing dead, diseased, and damaged growth. As much as possible, eliminate rubbing and crossing branches by removing the weaker or more damaged branch of the pair. Cut back other growth so that it is suitable for the size of the trellis. Don't be afraid to cut stems back hard to fit the support provided or to simply deal with tangled growth. The amount of material removed will depend on the size and vigor of the plant. While masses of twiggy growth can be chopped off with hedge shears or other similar tools, for the most part, handheld pruning shears are best. Use loppers or a saw for thick, woody stems.

When: With vines grown for their flowers, the best season for pruning a particular species depends on whether the species produces flowers on new wood (wood produced during the current year) or old wood (wood produced the previous year). Vines that bloom on old wood typically flower from late winter to early summer and are pruned in late spring or summer, immediately after flowering. Vines that bloom on new wood generally bloom from midsummer onward and are pruned in winter to early spring.

Framework Vine Pruning

For vines that are less vigorous, use a simple framework system. Train the vine by selecting several stems that will form a permanent framework. Look for stems that cover the entire trellis, and tie the framework stems in place as necessary.

Each time you prune, start by removing dead, diseased, and damaged stems, together with rubbing and crossing branches.

Also eliminate overcrowded shoots, unneeded shoots, and wayward stems that point in the wrong direction. Once the framework is established, look for side shoots that arise from each of the main framework stems. Cut these side shoots to within three or four buds of the main stem. This encourages strong, vigorous blooming wood. If one of the main framework stems begins to show signs of decline, replace it by training a new framework stem from the base of the plant.

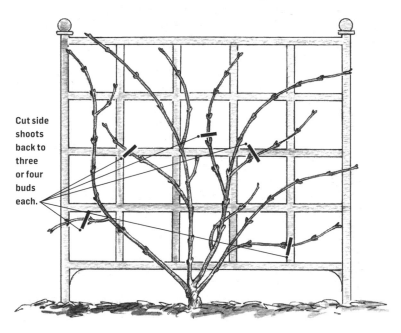

Cut side shoots back to three or four buds each.

FOR LESS RAMPANT VINES, both evergreen and deciduous, establish a framework of branches that covers the trellis.

Vine-by-Vine Pruning Guide

Use this list as a guide to pruning popular woody vines. In addition to popular vines that grace gardens everywhere, this list includes a number of species that have been designated as invasive but are still grown in gardens. Invasive plants are nonnative species that reproduce rapidly, have escaped cultivation, and are able to crowd out native plants in wild areas. Since these plants are still a part of a great many gardens, they are included here. While this section is not intended as a comprehensive list of invasive species, some of the worst offenders are indicated. Check with your local Cooperative Extension Service to find out which species are problematic in your area and to find out about less invasive species that are suitable for your area.

Actinidia **spp. (hardy kiwis).** Prune in late winter using basic vine pruning (page 105). If growing for fruit, use framework vine pruning (page 107). Cut back excessively long or wayward shoots in summer. Renovate if necessary by cutting back to the framework. Vines grown for fruit need more pruning. Fruit is borne on one-year-old shoots and at the base of new shoots produced during the current year, so prune out shoots that have already borne to encourage the formation of new ones. Establish a framework similar to grapes. Once the framework is established, cut back fruited vines to dormant buds each year to develop fruiting spurs. When growth emerges from the spurs in spring, pinch back the tips, leaving only five leaves on each shoot.

Akebia **spp. (akebias, chocolate vine).** Prune immediately after flowering using basic vine pruning (page 105). Invasive.

Ampelopsis brevipedunculata (porcelain berry). Use basic vine pruning (page 105) in spring. Invasive.

Aristolochia macrophylla (**Dutchman's pipe**). Prune in summer after flowering using either basic vine pruning (page 105) or framework vine pruning (page 107). Requires a strong trellis or other support. Plants can be pruned hard for renovation.

Bignonia capreolata (**crossvine**). Use basic vine pruning (page 105) immediately after flowering. Renovate plants in mid-spring, after the last frost date, by cutting them back hard into old wood.

Campsis **spp.** (**trumpet vine, trumpet creeper**). Prune using framework vine pruning (page 107) in late winter or early spring. Once established, plants can be cut back as hard as needed. Requires a strong trellis or other support. Renovate trumpet vines by cutting back a stem or two annually, or cut back the entire plant to within 1 foot of the ground. New growth will appear from the base.

Celastrus scandens (**American bittersweet**). Prune in late winter or early spring using basic vine pruning (page 105). Requires a strong trellis or other support. Renovate by cutting the oldest stems back to within 12 to 18 inches of the ground. Replace the old growth with new stems that arise from the base. Oriental bittersweet (*C. orbiculatus*) is invasive.

Clematis **spp.** (**clematis**). See box on page 111.

Cocculus carolinus (**Carolina moonseed, coral beads**). Prune in early spring using basic vine pruning (page 105).

Fallopia **spp.** (**formerly** *Persicaria* **spp.; mile-a-minute, silver fleece vine**). Prune hard in early spring using basic vine pruning (page 107). Invasive.

Pruning Clematis

Clematis are classified by bloom season and fall into three groups, each with different pruning needs. If you are not sure which group a plant falls in, and don't know the plant's name, observe it for a season to determine when it blooms and where on the plant the flower buds form. Sweet autumn clematis (*C. terniflora*) is invasive.

- **Early-flowering species/group 1:** These bloom from late winter to early spring on growth produced the previous year. *C. alpina, C. macropetala, C. montana,* and their cultivars are group 1 clematis. Prune immediately after flowering by removing dead and damaged growth. Cut stems back to fit the trellis or other support.

- **Early to midseason large-flowered cultivars/group 2:** These bloom from late spring to early summer and rebloom later in the season as well. Spring and early summer blooms are borne on side shoots that grow from old wood (stems produced during the previous season). Blooms borne from mid- to late summer are produced at the tips of the current season's stems. Prune group 2 clematis in early spring by first cutting out dead and damaged growth. Then cut back the main stems to a pair of healthy, vigorous buds. These produce the side shoots for the spring and early summer flowers, as well as the mid- to late summer display.

- **Late, large-flowered cultivars; late-blooming species; small-flowered clematis; and herbaceous species and cultivars/group 3:** This group is simpler to understand than its name implies. All of these clematis bloom in summer or fall on new wood (growth produced during the current season). Prune them in early spring, before growth begins; cut back stems until they are 6 to 18 inches above the soil surface. (Remove all above-ground growth on any clematis that are killed to the ground.) Cut just above a pair of healthy, vigorous-looking buds.

Gelsemium sempervirens (Carolina jessamine). Prune immediately after flowering using framework vine pruning (page 107). Carolina jessamines can be renovated by cutting one or more old stems back to the base of the plant, then replacing them with vigorous new stems.

Hedera spp. (ivies). Prune anytime using basic vine pruning (page 105). Remove any reverted growth that appears, meaning any growth with leaves that do not resemble the cultivar planted, or all-green growth on a plant that is variegated, for example. Ivies resprout readily from old wood. Renovate them by cutting back to a height of about 3 feet. Invasive.

Hydrangea anomala spp. *petiolaris* (climbing hydrangea). Prune after flowering using basic vine pruning (page 105). To renovate, prune in late winter or early spring. Prune plants back hard by removing stems using thinning cuts and cutting to the main framework branches. For best results, renovate over several years, since it will take plants several years to recover.

Jasminum spp. (jasmines). Prune immediately after flowering using basic vine pruning (page 105). To renovate, cut plants back to a height of 2 to 3 feet.

Lonicera spp. (honeysuckles). Use basic vine pruning (page 105) to prune honeysuckles. Prune common honeysuckle (*L. periclymenum*) in summer immediately after flowering. Prune Henry's honeysuckle (*L. henryi*), trumpet honeysuckle (*L. sempervirens*), trumpet honeysuckle cultivars (*L.* × *brownii*), and goldflame honeysuckle (*L.* × *heckrottii*) in late winter to early spring to control growth, remove weak shoots, and head back long stems. Renovate honeysuckles by cutting stems back to about 2 feet from the ground in winter or by cutting back a third of the oldest stems to the ground. Japanese honeysuckle (*L. japonica*) and its cultivars are invasive.

Mandevilla **spp. (mandevillas).** Prune in late winter or early spring using framework vine pruning (page 107). Mandevilla vines do not tolerate renovation.

Menispermum canadense **(Canada moonseed, yellow parilla).** Prune in early spring using framework vine pruning (page 107). Renovate every few years by cutting all stems to the ground in late winter.

Parthenocissus quinquefolia **(Virginia creeper).** Prune using basic vine pruning (page 105) in winter and/or summer. To renovate a Virginia creeper, cut back stems to within 3 feet of the base of the plant.

Passiflora **spp. (passionflowers).** Prune in early spring using either basic vine pruning (page 105) or framework vine pruning (page 107).

Schizophragma hydrangeoides **(Japanese hydrangea vine).** Requires minimal pruning. Prune, if necessary, in spring using basic vine pruning (page 105). If renovation is necessary, do it gradually over several seasons.

Vitis **spp. (grapes).** For covering an arbor or trellis, but not fruit production, prune in winter using basic vine pruning (page 105). Always cut just above a bud (look for a swollen leaf **node** if necessary). Grapes can also be managed using framework vine pruning (page 107) for a more controlled situation. For information on pruning grapes to produce fruit, see Pruning Grapes on page 115.

Wisteria spp. (wisterias). Japanese wisteria (*W. floribunda*) and Chinese wisteria (*W. sinensis*) both bloom on one-year-old wood. The main pruning objectives with both species are to develop blooming spurs and fight their rampant growth. Native American wisteria (*W. frutescens*) and Kentucky wisteria (*W. macrostachya*) are less vigorous and produce flowers on the current year's growth. Both also rebloom intermittently through the summer.

Train all wisterias on wires securely attached to a wall or an extremely sturdy trellis. During the first few years, develop lateral framework stems to correspond with the support. At planting, cut back the leader to 3 feet above the ground to encourage side branches, which can be tied to the framework. The first winter, cut back the side branches by one-third. Shorten all smaller branches (sublaterals) that arise from the main framework stems so that they have only two or three buds. Cut back the leader to encourage more side branches, if needed, and train new side branches to wires or other supports higher up.

Once the main framework has been established, prune annually in winter to shorten the main framework branches and also cut back all sublateral branches to two or three buds (3 to 4 inches). Asian species, especially, require annual pruning in summer, two months after flowering; cut back all shoots that are not needed to extend the plant's main framework. These shoots should be about 6 inches long and have only three to four leaves. Native wisterias can be renovated; cut them back to within 1 or 2 feet of the ground in winter. They also can be maintained as shrubs in this manner. Japanese wisteria (*W. floribunda*) and Chinese wisteria (*W. sinensis*) are invasive.

Pruning Grapes

Grapes are large, rampant vines that require severe annual pruning and a sturdy support in order to produce usable fruit. Pruning restricts both the quantity of vines produced as well as the number of bunches of fruit. Unpruned vines that are allowed to produce as much fruit as possible bear only small bunches that have tiny, unusable fruit. (It is still attractive to wildlife, though!) Grapes can be grown on an arbor or trellis, but plants grown for fruit production are typically grown on some type of post-and-wire trellis. All grapes bear fruit on new wood (growth from the current year) that arises from one-year-old wood.

GRAPES GROWN USING the curtain pruning system can be spaced anywhere from 5 or 6 feet apart to 8 to 10 feet apart. Prune the ends of the main framework vines annually in winter to keep adjacent plants from competing with each other.

A variety of pruning systems is available, and different systems are recommended for different types of grapes. (See Suggested Reading to find detailed information on pruning systems and trellising options.)

Curtain pruning is one simple system. Plant vines along a post-and-wire trellis, and start by establishing a main trunk. Let the main leader of the vine reach the top wire. In winter, to create the two main framework vines, cut the leader back to a strong side shoot just below the top wire and train that shoot along the top of the wire. Select a strong leader to run along the wire in the opposite direction. Allow side shoots to develop every 12 inches along each main framework vine. Remove vines that appear lower on the trunk. Each winter thereafter, cut the side shoots back to two or three buds. Remove shoots that arise from the bottom of the main framework arms and point downward. Each summer thereafter, cut all new side shoots back to a single leaf to keep them in check and prevent them from shading the grapes.

GLOSSARY

apical bud. The bud at the apex, or tip, of a shoot.

apical dominance. The controlling influence that the apical bud, located at the apex of a shoot, has on the remaining buds lower on the shoot. The apical bud grows most vigorously and releases auxins that inhibit the growth of buds lower on the stem.

bleeding. The leaking or oozing of sap from wounds or pruning cuts. While a little bleeding is not problematic, excessive bleeding can be. Minimize bleeding by pruning at the correct time for the plant.

branch angle. *See* crotch.

branch collar. The bulging or ringed area at the base of a branch. When pruning, cut just *outside* the branch collar to avoid damaging it.

bud. An undeveloped shoot, typically at the tip of a stem or along a stem. Buds may contain embryonic shoots, leaves, and/or flowers. On many plants, leaf buds and flower buds look different, with flower buds typically being larger than leaf buds. Buds that are alternate are borne one per leaf node on either side of a stem, while buds that are opposite are borne in pairs at leaf nodes on either side of a stem.

codominant stems. Two stems that have grown from the same stem and are growing at equal rates. Unlike branches, codominant stems do not have a branch collar. Instead, a ridge of bark develops between the stems. Codominant stems can form strong unions. U-shaped unions are stronger than V-shaped ones. If cracking or included bark exists between the stems, the union is weak and prone to breaking. It is best to eliminate codominant stems when training a young tree.

crotch. The angle formed when a branch grows from a tree. Also called branch angle. Wide crotches (45 degrees or more) are strongest.

crown lifting. Removing the lower branches of a tree to make room for pedestrians or other traffic. Also called limbing up and crown raising.

hard pruning. The meaning of this often-used term varies depending on the plant being discussed. It is used to describe pruning a shrub or other plant back to an existing framework as well as renewal-pruning to renovate a plant. "Hard pruning" is also sometimes used to recommend cutting a plant back more severely than it normally requires to eliminate excessive deadwood or old wood or to eliminate excessive overcrowded growth.

heading cut. A pruning cut made across a stem to remove the stem tip. *See* page 21.

included bark. Bark that has become incorporated into the joint between a branch and the trunk of a tree. Joints with included bark commonly arise from codominant stems or narrow crotch angles. They are typically much weaker than broader joints where bark has not grown into the joint.

leader. The main terminal shoot or trunk of a tree or the main shoot of a branch. A double or dual leader forms when two competing shoots arise. *See* page 54.

limb(ing) up. *See* crown lifting.

new wood. Growth produced during the current growing season.

node. The point on a stem where one or more leaves or buds are attached. Nodes are often referred to as "leaf nodes," although the buds in nodes can give rise to flowers or stems.

old wood. Growth produced during a previous growing season.

renewal pruning. Also called renovation or rejuvenation, renewal pruning is a process that uses thinning cuts to promote new, vigorous growth on shrubs or other woody plants by eliminating old wood. A plant can be renewed over the course of several years by removing one or more old stems. Other shrubs can be cut entirely to the ground in a single season for renewal. Renewal pruning can be used only on plants that will sprout from old wood; it will damage or kill those that will not sprout from old wood.

side shoot/sublateral. A shoot or branch that arises from a main or lateral shoot or branch.

stem. A main axis of a plant that has nodes and internodes and bears and supports the leaves, flowers, and other plant parts.

stub. A small section of branch left on a plant. Stubs can be left after improper pruning cuts or when a branch breaks off naturally.

sucker. A shoot that arises from the roots of a plant or from the crown or an underground stem. On grafted plants, suckers can arise from the rootstock, below the graft union; these are called root suckers. The term "sucker" is also used to refer to any fast-growing upright stem.

thinning cut. A pruning cut that removes a stem or branch at its base where it arose from a larger branch or the trunk of a tree. See page 14.

watersprout. A thin vertical or nearly vertical stem that arises from a branch. Watersprouts normally grow very fast, do not branch, and seldom produce flowers or fruit.

woundwood. Woody tissue that forms around wounds on trees, shrubs, and other woody plants.

SUGGESTED READING

Brickell, Christopher, and David Joyce. *The American Horticultural Society Pruning & Training*, rev. ed. DK Publishing, 2011.

Hill, Lewis. *Pruning Made Easy: A Gardener's Visual Guide to When and How to Prune Everything, from Flowers to Trees*. Storey Publishing, 1997.

Hill, Lewis, and Leonard Perry. *The Fruit Gardener's Bible: A Complete Guide to Growing Fruits and Nuts in the Home Garden*. Storey Publishing, 2011.

Martin, R. Sanford. *How to Prune Fruit Trees*, 20th ed. Echo Point Books, 2013. First published 1944.

Otto, Stella. *The Backyard Orchardist: A Complete Guide to Growing Fruit Trees in the Home Garden*. OttoGraphics, 1993.

Powers, Tom. *The Organic Backyard Vineyard: A Step-by-Step Guide to Growing Your Own Grapes*. Timber Press, 2012.

Proulx, Annie. *Great Grapes: Grow the Best Ever*. A Storey Country Wisdom Bulletin, A-53. Storey Publishing, 1980.

Reich, Lee. *The Pruning Book*, rev. ed. Taunton Press, 2010.

Rombough, Lon. *The Grape Grower: A Guide to Organic Viticulture*. Chelsea Green Publishing, 2002.

Metric Conversion Formulas

WHEN THE MEASUREMENT GIVEN IS	TO CONVERT IT TO	MULTIPLY IT BY
inches	millimeters	inches by 25.4
inches	centimeters	inches by 2.54
inches	meters	inches by 0.0254
feet	meters	feet by 0.3048
feet	kilometers	feet by 0.0003048

INDEX

Page numbers in *italic* indicate illustrations.